The Institute of
Business Ethics

The Institute of Business Ethics seeks to clarify ethical issues in business, to
propose positive solutions to problems and to establish common ground with
people of goodwill of all faiths. Its funds have charitable status, being separately
administered on behalf of its subscribers, by the founding body, the Christian
Association of Business Executives, Registered Charity No. 256182.

12 Palace Street, London SW1E 5JA
Telephone: 071 931 0495
Facsimile: 071 821 5819

First published 1994
by the Institute of Business Ethics
12 Palace Street
London SW1E 5JA

ISBN 0 9524020 0 9

THE INSTITUTE OF BUSINESS ETHICS

Rapid changes in the technology, methods and scale of business raise ethical issues to which legislation and experience cannot provide all the answers. Society is increasingly concerned and there is growing involvement with business ethics in political, academic and theological circles.

Business must be seen fully to share these concerns. There is also the need to promote practical solutions which combine social responsibility with efficient operations. Otherwise business can find itself fighting constant, rearguard actions against well-meaning but inappropriate solutions proposed by people not directly involved.

The aims of the Institute are to emphasise the essentially ethical nature of wealth creation, to encourage the highest standards of behaviour by companies, to publicise the best ethical practices and to demonstrate that business ethics involve positive initiatives, as well as constraints.

The Institute provides a forum for responsible policy formulation on these issues. It holds consultations and conferences, undertakes research and identifies effective actions which business enterprises can take. It offers practical advice to companies wishing to establish and implement effective ethical policies. It also represents responsible business opinion to the media and in the continuing public debate with academics, theologians and politicians.

The Institute of Business Ethics was launched before an audience of business leaders at the Mansion House in October in 1986 by the then Lord Mayor of London, Alderman Sir Allan Davis GBE, with the endorsement of the Archbishop of Canterbury, the Cardinal Archbishop of Westminster, the Moderators of the Free Church Federal Council and of the Church of Scotland, the Chief Rabbi and the Imam of the London Central Mosque.

In the past seven years the Institute has been well established, and commands widespread support, as is shown by the membership of its Council and its Patrons. "A list of the publications that have resulted from the research, surveys, conferences, seminars and consultations of the Institute are given in Appendix Four. "Benefiting Business & the Environment" is the third in a series on environmental issues, which the Institute has commissioned the Green Alliance to write.

THE GREEN ALLIANCE

The Green Alliance is an independent, non-profit-making organisation working on environmental policy. It aims to raise the prominence of the environment on the agendas of public and private institutions including Government, industry, finance, voluntary organisations and professional bodies.

Julie Hill joined The Green Alliance in 1985 and has been Director since November 1992. She has co-ordinated a broad range of projects with industry and environment components including work on pesticides, biotechnology and integrated pollution control, and has worked extensively on environmental legislation. She is author of "Towards Good Environmental Practice" (Institute of Business Ethics 1992) and co-author with Tom Burke of "Ethics, Environment and the Company" (Institute of Business Ethics 1990). She has a Masters degree in Politics from the London School of Economics and qualifications in ecology and conservation.

Ingrid Marshall has a degree in Human Environmental Science from King's College London and joined the Green Alliance in 1992. She has been Projects Officer since 1993 and has been responsible for work on sustainability in Government departments and on the EC's Fifth Action Programme on the Environment.

Catherine Priddey joined the Green Alliance in 1993 and is Assistant Projects Officer. During a year with Oxfam she worked on trade, development and the environment, and for the Green Alliance has covered corporate environmental reporting. She has a Masters degree in International Relations from the University of Bristol.

ACKNOWLEDGEMENTS

In addition to those companies named in the text, we would also like to thank the following for their help and advice:

Rod Aspinwall, Aspinwall & Company; Richard Bate, International Chamber of Commerce UK; Alex Bennett, the Automotive Consortium on Recycling and Disposal; Mark Campanale, National Provident Instutution; Cameron Clark, Department of the Environment; John Elkington, SustainAbility; Ian Harrison, Orr & Boss; Mike Harrison, Myra Henderson and Sophie Higman of the RSA Environment Management Unit; Stephen Joseph, Transport 2000; Marek Mayer, ENDS; Malcolm McIntyre, McIntyre Consultants; John Stambollouian, Department of the Environment; Steve Warshal, Greenpeace Business; Adrian Watts, PAYBACK Environmental Business Association.

FOREWORD

By Derek Wanless, *Group Chief Executive of the National Westminster Bank and Chairman of the UK Advisory Committee on Business and the Environment (ACBE)*

Few people in business in the 1990s can claim to be unaware of environmental issues. The environment is now a constant, if not always dominant, part of the political agenda. The positive role that business can play in securing a better environment is a recurring theme for trade associations, government departments and pressure groups, and there is a growing number of publications and fora to debate the issues. More and more people expect all UK institutions, including businesses, to take steps to improve their environmental performance.

Yet for many businesses the problem is getting started, particularly if survival is the most pressing consideration. This collection of case studies shows that environmental measures can save costs, sometimes with no outlay at all, and often through investments with short payback times. Perhaps most compelling, the case studies illustrate the kind of thinking that leads to business and environmental excellence. Thinking about quality, thinking about efficiency, looking for new uses for materials previously considered waste, taking ideas from people at all levels in the organisation, talking with suppliers - all these characterise the companies that have put themselves in a leadership position.

At NatWest we are addressing a wide range of issues through our environmental responsibility programme, and we are proud to have our efforts featured in three of the case studies here. Our business, and that of many of our customers, may well depend in future on the action we take now to conserve resources, clean up past pollution and prevent further problems. I commend these case studies to all businesses looking for practical examples which will help them to identify areas where they too can make progress in the short and medium term.

CONTENTS

INTRODUCTION

Introduction

by Neville Cooper,
Chairman of the Institute of Business Ethics

In 1992 UNCED, the Earth Summit in Rio, addressed two of the greatest moral issues of our time: environment and development.

Leading companies in many countries, including a large number in the UK, made public commitments to environmental improvement before Rio and many more have done so since then through initiatives such as the ICC Business Charter for Sustainable Development, the Chemical Industry's Responsible Care Programme and the CBI's Environment Forum.

It is true that many companies are vulnerable to pressures from an increasingly environmentally-aware public. It is also a fact that some companies hope that some proposed legislation might be rendered unnecessary through effective and timely voluntary improvements.

But the best companies also recognise that environmental improvement is a positive and logical extension of their wider corporate responsibility to society. In other words, they regard the subject as part and parcel of the increased attention being given to business ethics.

This has been recognised by our Institute which has published two books on this topic - "Ethics, Environment and the Company" (1990), which made practical recommendations for environmental management and "Towards Good Environmental Practice" (1992), which gives detailed case studies of companies putting the recommendations into practice.

One of the problems of achieving real progress in environmental improvement has been that companies of all sizes saw, quite rightly, that there were often costs involved. In a severe recession, it was hard for all, and especially the smaller companies, to absorb such costs in their businesses. Yet these costs are often higher for companies which take a short term view and merely react to new regulations with "end of pipe" solutions, rather than aiming for long term environmental excellence.

This book outlines some of the advantages, in business terms, of good environmental management.

There are examples of companies which have seen the business advantages of cost reduction by reducing energy consumption, cutting wastes and achieving lower transport costs - all fundamentals of traditional good management, but now spurred on by environmental considerations. We have shown that some of these cost savings can be achieved with minimum investment and therefore very rapid payback, and sometimes without any investment at all.

Some companies included have seen opportunities in improved manufacturing processes, or in creating new markets or improving market share with new products which are more beneficial to the environment. There will be many more such examples in the future.

The companies mentioned in this book are not all large. Numbers of employees range from 26 to 156,000. Many of them are not involved in obviously environmentally damaging activities. Nor are they all involved in manufacturing - many are in the service industry sector. Thus this book is of relevance to companies of every size and in every sort of business.

The common thread linking the companies featured here is a proactive approach to environmental management and a recognition that there are real benefits to be achieved. There are direct benefits to the bottom line and there are also benefits in terms of reputation, as good companies from which to buy, in which to invest and for which to work.

Thus this book sets out to show that ethical attitudes to the environment can also be good for business.

We are most grateful to the companies involved in this study without whom this publication would not have been possible. We thank them for their time and enthusiasm in sharing their experiences. Our thanks should also be given to Julie Hill, Ingrid Marshall and Catherine Priddey of the Green Alliance for their hard work in researching and preparing the text. The dedicated contribution of the Director and staff of the Institute has, of course, been invaluable. Sincere thanks are also due to The Department of the Environment who, once again, contributed towards the costs of research and publication.

EXECUTIVE SUMMARY

Summary

Benefits to the Bottom Line

Environmental initiatives can in many cases save money and help to improve profitability and competitiveness. The case studies in this book detail 70 environmental initiatives taken by 43 companies which have resulted in benefits to the bottom line, new product opportunities or increased market share. For some companies action has been prompted by current or anticipated regulatory requirements.

Vast Potential

The total annual savings represented by these case studies, which is a small sample of UK companies, is in excess of £10 million. The highest individual saving is £1 million. The average payback period is eighteen months, although some initiatives involved no capital outlay at all. Thus the potential for savings in the UK as a whole is vast.

Relevant to all Businesses

No activity is without environmental impacts, even if they are not all subject to laws and regulations. The case studies in this book feature manufacturing companies, retailers and service companies. The businesses range from very large to small - they have turnovers between £13.7 billion and £2.8 million and the number of employees ranges from 156,000 to 26.

The desire to save money applies to any business. For many of the companies featured here looking at environmental issues such as emissions and polluting wastes has brought home the unnecessary costs incurred by wastage of energy, water and raw materials and the final disposal of "waste" products. As one contributor put it, "It is staggering to think that so much money has been going down the drain..." (see page 29).

Good Thinking

These case studies illustrate the kind of thinking needed to reap the benefits. Thinking efficiency, thinking quality, looking for new uses for materials previously considered waste, taking ideas from people at all levels in the company, working with suppliers - all these characterise the companies that have put themselves in a leadership position.

Different Approaches

Industrial laundry firm **Spring Grove Services Ltd** are saving £30,000 annually on water and energy costs by simple process changes. A pupil from a local school thought up one of the ideas that will save around 1,000 gallons of water per year (see page 26).

The **National Westminster Bank Plc** made a comprehensive audit of the company's environmental impacts. Energy saving initiatives introduced in 1992 alone have saved them £630,000 per year. Simply cutting out one computer print-out has saved £42,000 (see page 31).

Hotel group **Forte Plc** saved £180,000 in 1993 alone by installing combined heat and power plants in 60 of their hotels (see page 15).

Pharmaceuticals company **Glaxochem Ltd** are saving approximately £1million a year by reducing losses of Volatile Organic Compounds (VOCs) (see page 35).

Acme United Limited, a company with 70 employees, has opened up a profitable market by developing nail scissors made entirely from recycled materials. Their product is marketed with strong environmental branding by Boots The Chemists (also featured here with large savings from packaging initiatives) (see pages 57 and 48).

Tissue paper makers **Scott Limited** expect to recover a £2 million investment in water treatment, prompted by water pollution regulations, in five years thanks to the recovery of water and previously wasted raw materials (see page 29).

Skippingdale Paper Products Ltd are saving £195,000 per year on transport costs by reducing the volume of disposable nappy packs by almost 60%. Lorry journeys have been reduced by 600,000 km a year (see page 51).

An alphabetical list of companies, details of their businesses and a summary of initiatives taken is in Appendix 1. Many of the contacts and publications used by these companies in formulating their successful strategies have been gathered together in Appendices 2 and 3.

WHY NOT TAKE ENVIRONMENTAL INITIATIVES?

Initiatives

There is no shortage of information as to why companies should pay attention to the environment. Evidence of continuing high public awareness of the issues, consumer pressure and existing or impending regulations from the UK and Europe - all these factors are highlighted regularly in surveys and reports.

This report has set out to demonstrate that there is a very important additional reason for taking environmental initiatives - they can also increase profits. Some of the projects and techniques discussed did not even arise from something called an "environment policy"- they were cost saving measures that also have clear environmental advantages. It does not matter which came first - the environmental consciousness or the cost-cutting - the net result is benefits on both counts.

Some of the cost-saving measures described here resulted from such simple changes that it is difficult to understand how they were not picked up by routine monitoring of the company's operations. Good environmental management is in many ways simply good management: paying attention to whether materials or energy are being wasted, considering how by-products can be re-used, making sure that operations are always run at maximum efficiency. If management practices in UK business are not improved, we will lag behind competitors in other countries environmentally as well as economically.

> *"no activity is without environmental impacts, even if they are not all subject to laws and regulations"*

Other than failing to recognise and address bad management, the apparent reasons for inaction include the following:

It doesn't apply to us. This is still the reaction of many companies, particularly small ones, to discussion of environmental issues. It is wrong for two reasons. One is that no activity is without environmental impacts, even if they are not all subject to laws and regulations. The other is that the need to save money applies to any business concern.

It's bound to be expensive. It could be expensive, but it's not bound to be. Some companies do face significant costs as regulations are progressively tightened and new technologies or far-reaching process changes are required to meet new standards. In some cases, however, these costs will be an investment that helps to save money in the long run, so that after a payback period they will contribute to a company's profitability.

If it ain't broke, don't fix it. Put another way, we've always done it like this, why change now? It can be difficult to see things with fresh eyes after several years' involvement with the same processs. This may be one of the reasons why adopting an "environmental programme" as a new context in which to look at a company's activities has in some cases yielded spectacular results. Such a process often means bringing members of staff together in new combinations, or perhaps involving outside consultants, who are likely to have a different perspective. The obvious is often overlooked.

> *"adopting an 'environmental programme' as a new context in which to look at a company's activities has in some cases yielded spectacular results"*

It's hard enough coping with today, let alone tomorrow. A short term viewpoint has been forced on some UK companies by recession and by financial institutions. With many companies struggling to survive, it is, of course, difficult to devote time to setting up and monitoring completely new management systems. Yet many of the initiatives described in this book were brought in piece-meal, and were no less effective for that. The important point is that the thinking that led to them could be extended into other areas as time and resources permit.

It is in companies' and the environment's interests to combat short termism. Immediate profit often seems to get more emphasis than long term viability. The projects described here have payback periods averaging 18 months - much longer and the likelihood is that some would never have been allowed to go ahead.

Once companies have decided to implement environmental initiatives, whether individually or as part of an action programme, the keys to success are measuring, monitoring and reporting. The message comes through time and time again in the case studies; many of those we interviewed say, in different ways, "If you can't measure, you can't improve". Monitoring and reporting are then essential to be able to show all stakeholders, including employees, management, investors, shareholders, the public and interest groups, what is being achieved. Ensuring that staff, in particular, have involvement in, and ownership of, environmental initiatives is crucial.

The chapters of the book reflect the main types of initiative that have led to cost savings, for instance, reductions in energy use, water use and waste generation. However, many initiatives will have produced benefits in more than one area, so the groupings of case studies under chapter headings are really only for guidance as to the primary goal of the initiative. We have also included chapters on improving market share and the benefits of working with suppliers, since under both headings we have found companies prepared to attribute business benefits to improvements in environmental performance.

> *"It is in companies' and the environment's interests to combat short-termism"*

COMPANIES FEATURED

Companies

Pages

1. USING LESS ENERGY

Less Energy

CASE STUDIES

Introduction

Energy use is an obvious area in which companies can look for cost savings. Energy saving also yields great environmental benefits because of the polluting effects of most sources of energy.

Burning **fossil fuels** such as oil, coal and gas, whether directly or to produce electricity, contributes to the build up of **carbon dioxide** in the Earth's atmosphere, and therefore potentially to climate change. Fossil fuels also give rise to **sulphur dioxide** and **nitrogen oxides**, the main components of acid rain. In most UK power stations only about one third of the energy in the fuel ends up as useful energy in the form of electricity, with the rest lost as waste heat. Nuclear power produces less carbon dioxide in operation, but building a nuclear power plant involves considerable amounts of fossil fuel and therefore CO_2. The problems involved in the disposal of radioactive waste and the possibility, however small, of a catastrophic accident, make it a controversial and, to some, unacceptable option. It would be desirable for **"renewable"** sources of energy such as wind power and solar power to form in the future a significant part of the energy mix, but at present they are not developed enough to be reliable. The Government does have a target of 1,500MW of new electricity generating capacity from renewable sources by the year 2000, and estimates that by 2025 renewables may supply between 5% and 20% of current UK electricity. Renewables can, however, have their own environmental impacts, such as the visual intrusion and noise associated with wind farms.

> *"The energy crises of the 1970s did much to encourage greater energy efficiency in industry but technologies and monitoring techniques, and thus the opportunities for savings, have improved even further in the last decade"*

Given these environmental penalties, and the financial benefits of using less energy and using it more efficiently, all companies should have an energy use reduction programme. The energy crises of the 1970s did much to encourage greater energy efficiency in industry but technologies and monitoring techniques, and thus the opportunities for savings, have improved even further in the last decade. The examples in this section demonstrate a number of different strategies, from simple changes in lighting design to investment in new technologies. They show that benefits can be realised very quickly.

Generation

Combined Heat and Power - the Most Efficient Form of Generation

Combined Heat and Power (CHP) installations tap the waste heat normally associated with electricity generation, enabling it to be used locally to heat water and buildings and industrial processes (CHP Association - see page 78).

The hotel group **Forte Plc** achieved savings of **£180,000** in 1993 by installing **CHP** plants in 60 hotels. The payback period on these installations is 2½-3 years. By 1995 Forte intends to have CHP units in a further 100 premises and expects to save, based on today's prices, each year, about £½ million.

Concern over its sizeable energy bill led Forte in 1983 to pioneer the first hotel CHP unit as part of an Energy Efficiency Office demonstration project. A CHP unit allows electricity to be generated on site, the waste heat being utilised to contribute directly towards water and space heating, replacing the heat of a conventional boiler. The trial period ran for three years at the end of which high maintenance costs were making the units uneconomic and the trial was ended.

Forte was prepared to field trial the second generation CHP only if someone else funded the project until the technology was proven. John Forte, Environmental Services Director, says "Our current supplier approached us in 1987 claiming to have overcome the reliability problems. They also came up with the idea of 'discounted electricity'. They said 'give us a space in your boiler house for us to put in our CHP unit and supply us with the gas to run the machine, and we will supply you with the major part of your hot water and heat requirements. In addition, you can buy the electricity produced at a lower price than you currently pay'. Hence there is no capital cost and no risk because we still have our full boiler plant and the grid supplying us with electricity if necessary. If the plant breaks down the only thing that happens is that the supplier does not get any money for his investment. The incentive for him is to keep the plant running as much as possible".

The CHP experiment has been one success but the company is exploring other options for reducing energy costs. Operations which are a long way from municipal sewage treatment works could have their own works on site. Forte is currently investigating the potential to use the biogas from such plants to generate energy.

At their waste water treatment works in Canterbury **Southern Water Services Ltd** is saving **£3,000 per month** on electricity following the installation of a **CHP** system.

For years, the company used bacteria to digest sludge in a large tank at most sites and the gas generated by the process, which is 60% methane, went to "flare", in other words, was burned off. The tank would be heated to the required temperature of 35°C by a separate boiler system. The company realised that the wasted methane gas could be used to heat the boiler, and it was then only another short step to using it to power an engine, which provides heat for the digester and electricity for the sites. Southern Water has been using CHP technology at one site since the 1940s but the decision to look at modern CHP systems was taken as part of a review of energy costs and methods of sludge digestion in 1989-90.

However, the development of an installation programme has been far from straightforward. The company experienced many problems with the first two modern engines they tried, thanks to an incompatibility between the engine and the corrosive qualities of hydrogen sulphide in the sludge. Learning from this experience, the engine chosen for Canterbury is based on a Victorian model, originally designed for use in oil fields where levels of hydrogen sulphide are high. This rediscovered technology has proved to be very successful.

The amount of heat from the engine is sufficient to keep the digester running and, through a small generator attached to the back, to produce 105 kilowatts of electricity which is used on site. Now, nearly 60% of all electricity needed is produced on site, saving £36,000 per year on importing electricity from the grid or the company's two main generators elsewhere. If there are any mechanical failures, the company can always fall back on the grid supply to keep the digestion process running.

Despite the programme's teething problems, Southern Water is planning to expand the use of CHP systems to all suitable sites over an unspecified period of years. The cost of installation at Canterbury was £180,000 and the payback period is not likely to be less than 5-6 years, but, as George Scarrott, Project Engineer, says, "It is the first engine of its type in Britain and is really a pilot scheme. But it is doing the job. Most companies prefer a 3-4 year payback but, at the end of the 5-6 years, we anticipate we will have an asset which could run on and on - at least for 35 years".

"Most companies prefer a 3-4 year payback but, at the end of the 5-6 years, we anticipate we will have an asset which could run on and on - at least for 35 years"

"This gas should
not be seen as
waste - it is an
asset"

Southern Water is now examining other means of powering their engine. Kent County Council has a full landfill site nearby which it is planning to cap and cover with a car park. Waste in landfill rots down, giving off a gas that is cleaner than the biogas and which can be mixed with it to give an even more suitable fuel to power the CHP engine. If the car park scheme goes ahead, the council will lay a pipe from the landfill site to the Southern's gas holder where the gases will be mixed. George Scarrott says, "Why waste energy or pollute the atmosphere when it can be put to good use? This gas should not be seen as waste - it is an asset".

Making a Corporate Commitment on Energy

The benefits to business of good energy management are the main focus of the UK Government's campaign "Making a Corporate Commitment".

At the Earth Summit, the Prime Minister pledged to reduce UK CO_2 emissions to 1990 levels by the year 2000. Fossil fuels are still largely used for electricity generation, a process which contributes significantly to CO_2 emissions and global warming. One kilowatt hour (kWh) of electricity thus generated emits one kilogram of CO_2 into the atmosphere. Cutting emissions from energy consumption will make important inroads into the reduction target. Although much research is now being undertaken into the use of renewable forms of energy, this will not provide an immediate answer to the problem. A much more readily achievable goal is that of energy use reduction.

The Energy Efficiency Office asserts that, up to a fifth - £10 billion - of the nation's fuel bill could be saved each year through increased energy efficiency.

The Making a Corporate Commitment campaign seeks board level commitment to energy efficiency as part of positive environmental management. It has drawn support from the Institute of Directors (IOD), the Confederation of British Industry (CBI), the Association for the Conservation of Energy (ACE) and many other influential organisations. Over 1,700 companies have so far signed the Declaration of Commitment which commits a company to seven guiding principles for an effective energy efficiency programme. These include publishing a corporate policy, establishing an energy management responsibility structure, setting performance targets, educating employees and reporting performance changes to stakeholders.

The campaign promotions point to the benefits of reduced running costs, improved public image and a healthier balance sheet, as well as the benefits to the environment: "Saving energy now means a better business and a better future".

(See Appendix Two for further information).

Energy from Rubbish

Blue Circle Waste Management Limited is exploiting an opportunity to establish an **alternative energy source**, and selling electricity to the national grid.

Blue Circle Industries plc extracts large quantities of minerals for its cement production. A normal part of the planning consent for quarrying is that the company has to restore the land after extracting material. Many of the disused quarries have been used as landfill disposal sites.

Until the early 1980s, the management of the sites was contracted out to others, but then Blue Circle Industries saw economic advantages in running the sites itself and established Blue Circle Waste Management Ltd (BCWM). Blue Circle Industries first exploited landfill gas in 1980 at its Norman Works followed by the commissioning of the Stone Gas Plant in 1986. Both schemes directly replaced fossil fuels as process heat.

> *"When you use the gas, you have an income with which to fund improvements..."*

In 1980 BCWM began experimenting with landfill gas. The processes that decompose organic wastes produce landfill gas, a mixture of mainly methane and carbon dioxide. Landfill operators have a statutory duty to prevent health and environmental risks from uncontrolled gas releases, and this has normally meant flaring, i.e. burning it. Methane, in its unburnt state, has a global warming potential several times that of carbon dioxide. When burnt, the methane converts to carbon dioxide which reduces the impact on the atmosphere, but is still adding to global warming. It is also very wasteful as landfill gas has about half the heating value of natural gas and can be burnt to provide heat or used to generate electricity.

BCWM decided to exploit this energy source and has installed generators at four sites. The company now has the capacity to produce nearly 10 megawatts (MWs) of electricity. Most of the electricity is sold to the national grid. A one-MW scheme, for example, would typically earn in the region of £450,000 per annum. BCWM also has one local customer for direct gas sales to whom it supplies approximately 2 million therms per year, charging him the equivalent of the price of the fuel replaced. In 1990, in recognition of its work to generate power from landfill gas, BCWM was voted overall winner of the energy conservation category of the Industry in Kent Environment Awards.

The cost of installing a one-MW generator is approximately £700,000. On the basis of the revenue from the electricity sold, the simple payback period would be 2-3 years, but the maintenance costs are considerable and increase the payback time to about 10 years. Few companies, including BCWM, would consider projects with such a distant return on investment. However, as a renewable energy source, the schemes qualify for funding under the Government's Non-Fossil Fuel Obligation (NFFO - see Appendix Four). The NFFO subsidy brings down the payback period to about 5 years, which is much more acceptable to the company, and encourages further investment. BCWM has recently registered further schemes under the NFFO which should generate another 6-7 MWs.

BCWM now exports sufficient electricity to the national grid to supply the domestic needs of a city the size of Salisbury, reducing substantially the need for output from conventional power stations. Dick Turner, Landfill Gas Operations Manager, says, "The overall effect is highly beneficial to the environment. That is why I feel the Government should subsidise such projects. If the subsidy was not there, the gas would simply be flared off to maintain the safety of the site. When you use the gas, you have an income with which to fund improvements to the system rather than a loss-making operation".

In the UK it is estimated that there is enough usable landfill gas to provide 650 MWs of electricity per year. Current schemes in the UK are generating only one tenth of this. The BCWM scheme could be repeated at other sites, helping to fulfil the Government's target of 1,500 MWs of new renewable electricity generating capacity by the year 2000.

Monitoring Energy Use - the Key to Savings

For **Triplex Safety Glass Ltd.**, the automotive glass manufacturers (part of the Pilkington Group), monitoring energy use has been the key to **instant savings**. The company has developed a **computer monitoring system** which tracks minute-by-minute use of electricity and gas. According to Roger Leeming, European Production Manager, "We have two UK sites that spend about £2 million each year on electricity. A 5% saving on that (i.e. £100,000) is virtually guaranteed simply by watching where the energy is used. Indeed, we hope to achieve a 10% saving on the amount budgeted for electricity for 1994". Installation costs were £50,000, meaning an expected payback of about 6 months. The system also monitors water use.

Triplex has also benefited from contract energy management. The company, First Energy, was paid a flat fee to provide Triplex's energy requirements, giving the incentive to maximise efficiency of fuel use. Savings extra to those contracted were shared. It replaced outdated heating equipment with more efficient technology and installed a monitoring system to ensure that the equipment was being used optimally. Roger Leeming says, "The system has only been running for a year, so it is too early to have detailed cost savings, but we believe that it has worked better than our expectation of a 30% reduction in gas usage over a year. The major advantage is that the contract company took the risk of replacing equipment, which was something that we would not have given priority to as an item of capital expenditure".

Blue Circle Industries Plc saves **3-5% of its annual energy costs** at plants where it has installed **computerised control systems** in its cement kilns.
After obtaining two Government grants in the early 1980s, Blue Circle linked up with the Scientific Instrument Research Association to develop a computerised "expert" system which would give finer control over the kiln burning process. The aim was to reduce fuel costs and emissions, particularly of oxides of nitrogen (NO_x) which were already an issue in Japan and which Blue Circle anticipated would be in the UK. The result was the LINKman system.

LINKman works by analysing temperature and gas composition in several areas of the kiln system, and controls these by adjusting the materials and fuel feed taken to the kiln and the volume of air drawn in for combustion. By constantly monitoring these parameters, the system can optimise process efficiency.

When a kiln is operated manually, adjustments are normally made to the kiln process every 30 minutes to an hour. LINKman reviews conditions once a minute and can make smaller adjustments more frequently and consistently. This avoids overheating the kiln, ensures efficiency of combustion and hence, produces lower gaseous emissions and wastes less fuel. For example, if the burning zone temperature is too hot, LINKman takes fuel off to let it cool down to optimum conditions. A significant spin-off benefit from this is that the quality of the clinker produced in the kiln is improved. If the material is overheated in the burning zone, the clinker becomes very dense and harder to grind in the cement mills, using more electrical energy in the process. LINKman prevents this.

At the first site in which LINKman was installed, **fuel savings of £500,000 per year** (7.7%) have been achieved. At the same time, reductions in NO_x across all sites average 40%, and in carbon monoxide (CO), 60-70%. Emissions of oxides of sulphur (SO_x) are also reduced and new technology is being installed to achieve accurate measurements of this benefit. The typical payback period for the LINKman installation is $1\frac{1}{2}$ years.

As a result of Blue Circle's environmental improvements, the company has been upgraded in B&Q's environmental supplier ratings (see page 68). Blue Circle is hoping this will translate into increased sales. In addition, in 1987 the company received a Better Environment Award for Industry for the development of LINKman.

> *"A 5% saving... is virtually guaranteed simply by watching where the energy is used"*

Lawrie Evans, Chief Chemical Engineer, explains the benefits of looking ahead and developing new ideas at the company's own pace, "As a result of the progress we have made in terms of management of the kiln process, our system has become the accepted standard and this will avoid our having to make the large amounts of capital investment being faced by some other cement companies to bring their plants into line".

This type of computerised control system is applicable not just within the cement industry, but to any company operating a rotary kiln system. It is currently used by companies in sectors such as petrochemicals and glass manufacturing, which can also benefit from improved monitoring and increased efficiency of their production processes.

Lighting - Often the Last Consideration

A **Coats Viyella Plc** garment hanging warehouse has saved over **£12,000 a year** through installing a redesigned and **efficient lighting system**, with a three year payback. Energy consumption was reduced by 66%. The warehouse had not been purpose built and the lights ran at right angles to the garment racks, leaving a lot of aisles in darkness. Lights were realigned to run along the individual aisles and each fitting incorporated three high-performance reflectors allowing the existing triple tube to be reduced to a single tube. The quantity and quality of lighting has improved dramatically.

> *"...initiatives with environmental benefits can be very simple..."*

Bluecrest Convenience Foods Limited has benefited from operating a **modern energy-efficient plant** since 1990. Even so, energy management experts were able to identify a further, significant improvement that could save the company money.

Bluecrest used 100 sets of double tube fluorescent lights in its building and it was suggested that if the company installed mirrors in place of one of the tubes, it could operate on single lights, cutting costs in half. After successful trials the mirrors were installed at a cost of £2,500. The savings made in energy amount to **£2,500 per year**, giving a payback period of one year, plus the benefit of 100 spare tubes to use as replacements, worth an estimated £250.

The costs savings achieved here demonstrate that initiatives with environmental benefits can be very simple and need not always involve large capital investment costs or complicated process changes.

Designing for Efficiency

For **Lloyds Bank Plc**, energy conservation is a major consideration both in the design stages for new buildings and in normal commercial use. Lloyds Bank has undertaken an impressive project in **energy efficiency** in its new Head Office building in Bristol which has enabled it to sell electricity to the national grid to the value of **£10,000 over a four month period** in the winter of 1993-4.

The building was designed as a low energy building and, after a reasonable period of occupation, will be assessed under the BREEAM scheme (Building Research Establishment Environmental Assessment Method - see page 87), in which the environmental performance of new buildings is assessed at the design stage. A CHP co-generation plant was installed with the aim of providing back-up to normal services. But it was soon realised that if the system was run at full capacity in peak periods, enough electricity could be produced to power the Bank's site, with the additional benefit of generating a large enough surplus to sell to the national grid. At the same time, the heat produced from the running of the CHP diesel engines is cycled back into the plant. Energy wastage is kept to a minimum as the site's requirements are measured every quarter of an hour, enabling the plant to shut down when its use is not economic.

A further cost benefit to Lloyds Bank comes from its position adjacent to the former Bristol Docks. Water is drawn in from the dock to use as a heating and cooling source. In the winter, water is warmer than surrounding air, so it can be passed through a heat exchanger which draws off the heat from the water to use as an additional heat source. The cooled water is discharged back to the dock. By the reverse process, in the summer, when the water is cooler than the surrounding air, it works as a cooling air conditioning system. By using this method, the Bank has a much reduced need for expensive gases and energy consuming cooling towers and compressors, and maintenance costs are significantly reduced. Only a small energy input is needed to cycle the harbour water.

According to Hugh Stebbing, Managing Director of Lloyds Commercial Properties Ltd, it is impossible to quantify the benefits of each aspect of the system as it is integrated into the overall building design, making the whole site extremely energy efficient.

Bluecrest Convenience Foods Limited is optimising its use of energy in its chilled and frozen meals plant in North Wales. Building on its experience of introducing energy efficiency measures at another, older site, it used the building of a new plant in 1990 as an opportunity to develop its ideas, with the benefit of being able to look at every aspect of building design.

The factory uses several compressors in its chilling and freezing systems. The heat generated from the process of compressing ammonia, which is used as a refrigeration gas, is piped through a tank where it heats water to a temperature of 55°C for handwashing and equipment cleaning. The only additional input of energy is provided by two gas boilers which heat water to 90°C for sterilisation purposes and steam for cooking. The heat recovery system is so efficient that at times slightly more is produced than can be used.

By using this **heat recovery** system, Bluecrest estimates that it has saved **£60,000 per annum**.

The Potential of Heat Exchangers

Spring Grove Services Ltd expects to save **£12,000 on its current fuel bill** when the full benefits of setting up a **heat exchanger system** are realised.

Spring Grove Services washes 34,000 wash-room roller towels per week and dries them on a "drying stack". In the drying process, the towels are driven over large steam cylinders to extract all the moisture. The extracted heat, steam and condensation used to be passed out through ventilators into the roof to the atmosphere. Spring Grove saw the possibility of using this wasted heat.

The company is installing a heat exchanger system in which the outgoing hot moist air will be used to heat copper plates as it passes through to the atmosphere. Dry air will be taken in from outside, passed by the reverse side of the plates, when it will be heated up and used to heat the factory. This system should satisfy all the factory's heating requirements except in very cold weather.

The installation of the necessary equipment cost £57,000, and Spring Grove anticipates a yearly saving of £12,000 on its energy costs. The payback period for the initiative is therefore 4-5 years. The use of waste heat as an energy resource is an initiative which could be adapted to many industry sectors.

A company in the carpet division of **Coats Viyella Plc** is saving **£25,000 per year** simply by **extracting heat from cooling water**, via a heat exchanger, which is then used to warm water for use in another process. The installation has paid for itself in one year. Communication of this achievement from the centre has meant that the idea is catching on in other subsidiary companies. Mike Lawford, Group Environmental Co-ordinator, says, "Monitoring energy consumption and losses raised the questions which led to this initiative, and others like it, getting off the ground".

A Comprehensive Strategy

In 1991 the **National Westminster Bank Plc** issued its energy policy with a target to reduce energy consumption for the group worldwide by 15% by 1995, taking 1990 as the base year. UK premises account for approximately 75% of the group's energy consumption. Stephen Herridge, the Bank's Principal Engineer, is confident that the target will be met through measures such as installing more energy-efficient equipment, improved standards of housekeeping and by incorporating energy-efficient design during building or refurbishment. As a result of implementing 350 initiatives in the largest UK premises in 1992, overall group energy consumption was reduced by 2.4%. Financial savings are estimated to be in the region of **£630,000 per annum**. Payback periods range from one month to three years, with the average around 10 months.

In 1992 the Bank collected energy data from its 500 largest UK properties which represent 40% of energy costs for the group. This enabled the identification of premises with high energy consumption per unit floor area. Energy audits were conducted at a number of these premises resulting in recommendations for investment. In a number of buildings it was found that the periods during which heating and air conditioning were in operation needed adjusting to ensure that energy was not being wasted when buildings were not occupied. In making the necessary changes, the only costs incurred were to cover the maintenance contractor's time. Some boilers were fitted with "delayed thermal response controllers" that improve efficiency when operating at part load in spring and autumn. Other simple initiatives included the fitting of thermostatic valves to individual radiators. These shut down the radiators when the surrounding air reaches a pre-set temperature.

"...a 66% reduction in lighting load..."

Typical lighting initiatives include replacing tungsten lightbulbs with compact fluorescent fittings at larger premises. In many premises twin tube fluorescent light fittings have been replaced with single more efficient tubes and a reflector. High frequency control systems were installed at the same time to increase further the efficiency of tubes. They also improve the working environment by eliminating flickering. "This resulted in a 66% reduction in lighting load in one 16,000 square metre building. Installation was in 1992 and savings amount to approximately £108,000 per annum", says Stephen Herridge. Coupled with staff awareness campaigns, additional switching has been installed in certain premises to split large expanses of lighting into zones, enabling staff to switch off particular areas when not in use.

Significant savings have been achieved in some of the Bank's largest administrative buildings through the installation of computerised building management systems. Using a series of sensors, heating, air conditioning and other building services can be monitored and controlled according to temperature changes throughout the day. Lighting can also be controlled. At an administrative centre in Birmingham the management system reduced gas consumption by 30% in 1992.

The Bank has continued to undertake similar initiatives although the financial savings have not been as great as from those implemented in 1992, which targeted investments that would give a higher and faster return. "It is common to tackle the easier things first and then move on to initiatives with longer paybacks", says Stephen Herridge. Another 300 initiatives implemented in 1993 are saving an estimated £300,000 per annum, reducing overall group energy consumption by a further 1-2%. The Bank still sees room for additional cost effective improvement. "We are currently considering energy targets for the 1996-2000 period", says Stephen Herridge, "Technology and management systems are continually improving, so there is always something new around the corner".

An important element of future savings will also be concentrating on the small branches, which constitute the majority of the Bank's 3,400 buildings in the UK. "Each site has a relatively low energy spend, making it difficult to justify individual energy audits", says Stephen Herridge. "We are currently introducing a novel system to overcome this problem. Maintenance contracts cover most of our UK properties and now, during routine visits to small branches, contractors also complete an energy questionnaire. These are analysed by an energy consultant who will make recommendations for investment without needing to visit the site." As a result the Bank expects to be making a large number of small investments - in thermostatic radiator valves and insulation, for example.

Esso Petroleum Company Ltd is a major energy user. Refineries consume the most energy and plants are designed with energy efficiency in mind. For instance, heat exchangers are widely used at refineries to transfer heat from hot products which need cooling to cooler products which need heating. CHP boilers are also used to harness the waste heat from processes. A typical refinery consumes in the region of 600 tonnes of steam per hour and at most sites the majority of this steam is provided by CHP boilers. Waste heat from steam-making is then tapped to produce electricity to meet almost all of a site's needs.

Other energy savings have been achieved through staff commitment. For instance, in 1993 a petroleum distribution terminal in Glasgow, employing around 20 staff, saved an estimated **£1,500** by reducing electricity consumption through the use of **photocells** on external flood-lights and a **"switch off" campaign**. The payback period on installing photocells was approximately 16 months.

The Glasgow initiative was driven by concern about the terminal's sizeable energy bill as well as moves towards increasing staff involvement in the running of the business. "It was very much a bottom-up process. Whilst discussing the pressures on the terminal's budget, two or three members of staff, plus the Operations Supervisor, agreed that a lot could be done to reduce electricity consumption. The plant manager was fully supportive and provided them with the resources they needed", says Ken Duggan, Regional Plant Manager.

Photocells were fitted to all of the external floodlights. These detect when light has fallen below or risen above set levels, switching lights on or off accordingly. Strategically placed on light switches and appliances, stickers with cartoons encourage staff to switch off when not in use. According to Ken Duggan, "With a campaign like this you have to motivate the person whose finger is going to be on the switch. The team at Glasgow felt they knew the best way to approach their own colleagues who were, in turn, more enthusiastic about it because the idea had come from their friends, rather than from the top".

"...motivate the person whose finger is going to be on the switch"

2. USING LESS WATER AND REDUCING POLLUTION

Less Water CASE STUDIES

Introduction

This chapter is about the consumption of water as well as about the problems of water pollution. It is often assumed that the UK has as much water as it needs, but in the late 1980s severe shortages in some parts of the country after a series of dry winters showed that supplies are by no means inexhaustible. The UK Government's main environmental policy document says that "the present margin between developed resources and demand may be uncomfortably narrow". It is also very difficult to predict future demand.

Shortages of water, even if temporary, are more than just a nuisance. Rivers dry up, or flow becomes so low that wildlife cannot be supported. The effects can be permanent and irretrievable. In the long term, the viability of industries and the security of supply for householders could be threatened by over-use of water.

The Aire and Calder Project

The Aire and Calder Project was established in the catchment area of the rivers Aire and Calder in Yorkshire in March 1992. Initiated by the Centre for Exploitation of Science and Technology (CEST), the project was supported by Her Majesty's Inspectorate of Pollution (HMIP), Yorkshire Water Services, The BOC Foundation for the Environment and the NRA, to demonstrate the benefits of adopting preventive measures of waste minimisation and cleaner technology. The focus of the Project is liquid effluent management.

The 11 companies taking part in the Project have a common interest as they all discharge to the same river system either directly, or indirectly via a sewage treatment works. Some of them also take water from the river for use in their processes.

In total over 500 options for improving efficiency have been identified. Many are extremely simple and have been implemented almost immediately. One company identified a 2.5% saving in water use on the first day. Perhaps the most important aspect of participating in the Project has been that companies have become more aware of the real costs and impacts of their processes. 40% of the measures identified could be classified as simply "good housekeeping" and a further 40% involved mostly straightforward modifications to technology.

The two participating companies featured in this book, Spring Grove Services Ltd and Lambson Fine Chemicals Ltd, are both keen to praise the results of the Project. In the first 18 months the 11 companies made total savings of £2.2 million per year, with a further potential of £2.2 million per year. The success of the Aire and Calder Project proves that reductions in pollution and improvements in profitability are not mutually exclusive.

Water costs money. So for environmental and cost reasons use of water, like energy, should be subject to a reduction programme. The case histories that follow demonstrate some very successful approaches.

Water pollution also costs money. The National Rivers Authority (NRA) charges for consents to discharge effluent, and costs vary according to the nature and quantity of the discharge. Immediate savings can be realised by "closing the loop", in other words re-using or recycling materials that would otherwise end up in waste water.

Finding Ways of Re-using Water

Since autumn 1992, the **Bayer Rubber Business Group** plant of Bayer plc has been saving **15-20% per year** on its water bill, by **recycling process water** for low-grade use.

Concerned about rising water costs, the company looked first at reducing water consumption on site through efficiency measures. An awareness campaign amongst staff and simple housekeeping measures such as new nozzles on hoses led to some success, although a little sporadic, but water usage remained high and the company decided to look at the possibilities for recycling.

"Although the motivation for making changes was purely economic, the idea of using as little clean water as is really necessary and re-using wherever possible, is an environmental principle that can be integrated into many processes"

The company manufactures synthetic rubber latex for the carpet, textile and paper finishing industries, a process which involves the treatment of effluent on site. After treatment, all final effluent water, which is only slightly contaminated, used to be discharged to the local brook under consent from the NRA. However, the company has a reservoir used by the previous site occupants, and decided to make use of this resource. Effluent water is now pumped to the reservoir and 15-20% is drawn off for low-grade use, such as floor and equipment washing and general cleaning. Ronan Vance, Works Engineer, says, "We use a lot of water for that kind of activity, so why pay a lot for good quality drinking water and use it to wash the floor? It would be a waste".

The cost of connecting pipework to the reservoir and pumping station and separating the mains for the two water supplies was £30,000. Payback was achieved in 1½-2 years. Bayer cannot re-use the water in its manufacturing as the treatment process makes the water very hard and it needs to be soft. The cost of re-softening it would be uneconomic, so the company is concentrating on further possibilities for use of recycled water.

Although the motivation for making changes was purely economic, the idea of using as little clean water as is really necessary and re-using wherever possible, is an environmental principle that can be integrated into many processes.

"Half the battle is being able to measure wastage. Then you have the opportunity to reduce it"

Through a combination of **recycling heated water** and improved monitoring of water consumption **The Standish Co**, a Coats Viyella subsidiary company, is saving in excess of £100,000 per year on energy and water processing costs. Standish began monitoring water and steam usage whilst participating in a "best practice" project, led by the Textile Finishers Association, aimed at minimising waste. The project, completed in July 1993, received support under the Department of Trade and Industry's Environmental Management Options Scheme (DEMOS). Monitoring was identified as crucial. "Half the battle", asserts Mike Lawford, Group Environmental Co-ordinator, "is being able to measure wastage. Then you have the opportunity to reduce it".

In one process incoming raw water requires filtration, softening and steam heating. The installation of a pump and piping to recycle hot wash water from the bleaching section to the scour wash section in the cotton treatment process has reduced water consumption by 40%, with no detrimental effect on quality. This has led to savings of £13,000 per year on water processing costs, and £37,000 per year on energy to raise steam. The payback period on capital investment was approximately one month.

In another initiative, the input of washing water to bleaching and cotton mercerising machines used to be manually controlled. By installing flow control valves calibrated to consume precisely the amount of water required to achieve best technical performance, water consumption has been drastically reduced. Annual savings on water filtration, heating and softening costs have amounted to £50,000. Capital investment was recouped in just under six months.

"the uninspected inevitably deteriorates"

Standish obtains raw untreated water for use in these processes from a nearby lake. It is extracted free of charge on the proviso that it is ultimately treated and returned to the river system. Had the water been treated and supplied, at a charge, by a water company, the costs, and therefore the savings, would have been much greater.

Coats Viyella Group has an environmental policy which covers its subsidiary companies and which is monitored through annual self audit questionnaires. Questions include resource consumption and wastage. Mike Lawford says, "We work by the maxim that 'the uninspected inevitably deteriorates'. Since starting the self audit many of our companies are starting to feel the benefits. Things that might have been acceptable, such as built-in waste factors, are no longer regarded as such and will be targeted for reduction".

Water-use Reduction Technologies

Spring Grove Services Ltd is saving **£30,000 per year** on its **water and energy costs** by introducing a series of changes to its cleaning process.

Following an invitation to become involved in the Aire and Calder Project (see page 24), the company looked at all areas of potential waste. The decision to attempt water reductions at source was not an easy one, because of the scale of investment needed and the lack of certainty on the payback period.

Part of Spring Grove's activities involve washing 34,000 wash-room roller towels per week. Water consumption here was reaching 810 gallons per hour, sprayed through 120 2.5mm diameter spray jets. The programme objective was to achieve acceptable washing standards whilst reducing water volume.

After considerable experimentation, the company installed a gate valve in the pipe for incoming water, in order to control the water flow rate from the pump, and replaced the spray jets with smaller aperture jets of 1.25mm, which maintained the spray pressure whilst reducing the volume of water used. The next step was to reduce the speed of the impeller in the water pump. By doing this, the gate valve could be removed and the flow of water controlled by the reduced pumping action.

Spring Grove has further plans for reducing water consumption, the main one being the installation of a sump tank to collect the final rinse water from the 13 washing machines used on site. In addition to the towels, the company washes over 40,000 garments, 10,000 pieces of "flatwork", such as cloths, and 8,000 mats per week. As in a domestic washing machine, the final rinse water is almost clean because a machine will pump in a lot of water to neutralise the remaining detergent. The company intends to use the last rinse water from three washing machines as the first water for five. The water will be dropped via a drain valve into a sump tank and pumped into an overhead storage tank ready for filling the machines with first wash water. This will reduce water intake by 68,000 gallons of water per year, saving the company more than £7,000, or a further 10% of Spring Grove's total water costs.

On a smaller scale, Spring Grove has recently started collecting the rainwater from the roof of one of its buildings and is piping it from the gutter straight into the sump tank. It is estimated that this will save around 1,000 gallons per year. The idea for this initiative came from a member of a local girls' high school which has been involved in looking at environmental issues at Spring Grove's site. Mark Lowe, Engineering Manager, says, "We are linking with the school to explore green issues. They benefit from the chance to examine industry and the environment, and we benefit as they are looking at ways we can make improvements".

> *"We are linking with the school to explore green issues. They benefit from the chance to examine industry and the environment, and we benefit as they are looking at ways we can make improvements"*

Reducing water usage is an ongoing process for Spring Grove. Mark Lowe says, "It all stemmed originally from the Aire and Calder Project, which has been a really worthwhile thing to be involved in. We have achieved a lot since we started 2 $\frac{1}{2}$ years ago, but the trick is now to try and keep it going and keep looking for ways to improve".

Better Effluent and Water Management

Bluecrest Convenience Foods Limited saved **£60,000** within a year of initiating an **improved effluent management process** at its chilled and frozen meals plant in North Wales.

In 1991, the company was sending two tanker loads (or 30 tonnes) of sludge to landfill per week at a cost of £52,000 a year, and spending £50,000 a year on chemicals to separate solids from the effluent stream at its on-site treatment plant. Faced with these high costs and a shared objective with Welsh Water to reduce its Chemical Oxygen Demand (COD) in order to meet consent levels, the company decided to establish a Waste Management Working Party to examine the problem.

It was discovered that the high COD level was due mainly to starches produced from the cooking of rice and potatoes, and that large quantities of food particles were ending up in the waste stream. A programme of staff education was introduced, raising awareness of the problem and encouraging careful management in the cooking process. This avoided food particles getting into the liquid waste stream, and also reduced overall amounts of waste. By this programme alone, sludge dropped from two tanker loads per week to one, involving a total saving of £25,000 over a year.

> *"Good environmental management is simply good management applied to environmental issues... we have proved to ourselves that environmental enhancement also makes sound business sense"*

The reduction in the amount of effluent produced also meant less chemical treatment was needed. This, combined with a change of chemicals used, produced a further saving of £35,000 over one year.

Having achieved such substantial savings with no capital investment, Bluecrest was spurred on to look further at its effluent management. As Richard Hallett, Production Director, says, "We did not envisage the next stage at all. We could have said, 'yes, we have done what is necessary' and stopped there. But once you get into something like this it has its own momentum and it snowballs". For a company with expertise in microbiological issues, the knowledge that the problem was mainly starches quickly led to a realisation that the effluent could be treated biologically. £40,000 was invested in a biological treatment unit, which consists of a large tank into which the effluent is pumped continuously. It is kept for 2-3 days whilst bacteria feed on the natural organic materials, reducing the COD level. The effluent then passes to the chemical unit for the final stage of treatment, after which the sludge is "clean" enough to use as agricultural fertiliser. Payback for the unit was achieved in one year.

However, in a further step, the sludge from the final stage is now fed back to the biological treatment tank and the bacteria feed on it again. Bluecrest now only needs one tanker every six weeks to take away the sludge - disposal costs have therefore reduced from £52,000 a year to approximately £4,000.

The alternative to this whole process was to simply increase the capacity of the chemical treatment unit and use more chemicals to treat the effluent. Whilst this would have reduced COD levels, it was neither an environmentally beneficial, nor an economically sound option. A keen awareness of environmental issues permeating through from the parent company, Booker Plc, encouraged a more responsible approach. For Richard Hallett, "Good environmental management is simply good management applied to environmental issues. At Bluecrest we have proved to ourselves that environmental enhancement also makes sound business sense. The key, as in all business, is to make a start. It is never as difficult as it appears".

Spring Grove Services Ltd is anticipating a **reduction in its effluent discharge costs from £200 per day to zero.**

As part of the Aire and Calder Project (see page 24) the company has examined all aspects of its processes for potential economic and environmental savings. In the case of effluent reductions, an added incentive to act has arisen from a change in Yorkshire Water discharge consent levels, imposed by the NRA.

Spring Grove cleans wash-room towels, work garments, mats and flatwork items such as cloths, and discharges water containing detergent and waste solids from the washing process. The company currently pays 45p for each cubic metre of effluent that goes to sewer. Engineers are experimenting with injecting carbon dioxide into the water to neutralise the pH before discharge. The system requires a settling tank large enough to hold one hour's volume of water, as the process of treating the effluent takes this amount of time.

Initial test results are encouraging and Spring Grove hopes ultimately to be able to put clean water straight into the adjacent River Calder, at no cost. Mark Lowe, Engineering Manager, says, "People automatically think that green issues mean huge capital outlay, whereas we are proving that they don't. There is money to be made in this".

"People automatically think that green issues mean huge capital outlay, whereas we are proving that they don't"

Over a period of 3 years, up to the end of 1993, the **Arjo Wiggins Fine Papers Limited** paper mill in Dover has reduced both water consumption and losses of raw materials in effluent ("drain losses") by almost 50%. This has given rise to cumulative savings on effluent charges and raw materials costs of **£120,000** and **£150,000** respectively.

Paper manufacture is highly water intensive. For Arjo Wiggins the key to reducing water consumption and drain losses, which are composed of cellulose fibres, chalk and starch, lay in **monitoring and targeting** (M&T). "You can only target improvements when you can accurately monitor. Through an in-depth knowledge of our water systems, metering the water and analysing the effluent we know how much water and raw materials we use and lose", says the mill's Process Development Officer, Kevin Clay. The Technology Services Manager, Keith Barr, views monitoring over the right time period as essential. "We used to report weekly on water consumption and drain losses. Now it is daily, enabling us to react promptly to unexpectedly high consumption or losses. It is this frequency of reporting that has driven our water consumption and materials loss levels down and held them down." The mill plan for the year contains targets for reducing water consumption and drain losses. "We make sure that the targets we set are challenging but achievable", says Keith Barr. The mill has a continuous programme to identify investments which will reduce the usage of fresh water and increase the potential to recycle it. Such investments have already given rise to significant reductions in total water used.

The mill has set out to minimise the use of fresh water. Consumption was significantly reduced when the mill's old water piping was replaced to prevent rust contaminating the paper. The new piping system was specifically designed to allow easier management and maintenance, which has proved essential to enabling prompt action to be taken in response to water losses. Staff involvement at all levels has also been crucial in reducing consumption. Keith Barr says, "Making staff more aware has encouraged them to be more vigilant in checking for areas where water is wasted. It is becoming part of their daily routine. We make sure that staff in the mill know how much water and money we are saving. This makes everyone work harder to meet future targets. It is self-perpetuating".

The mill also aims to maximise the recycling of used water. A lot of cooling water used to be discharged from the mill. "This was wasteful as it was clean, now we recycle it", says Keith Barr. Water that has been used in cooling is mixed with water from the paper-making process for re-use. Chalk, which gives paper its opacity, and fibres are recovered and separated so that they can be re-introduced into the paper-making process. The mill's vacuum pumps used to be sealed with fresh water, now recycled water is used. The mill only produces variants (or "grades") of white paper. Previously, when switching from one grade to another all of the water which had been used to produce a particular shade was replaced. By ensuring that grades, which run naturally together, follow on from each other the same water can now often be re-used for the next grade.

> *"Making staff more aware has encouraged them to be more vigilant in checking for areas where water is wasted"*

In addition to recycling and reducing the usage of fresh water, losses of fibre, chalk and starch (applied to improve the strength and printability of the paper) have been significantly reduced through improving the control of their retention in the paper. This has been achieved through using a new "chemical retention aid" more effectively. This has not only significantly reduced raw materials consumption but it has also improved the quality of the mill's effluent.

Arjo Wiggins is committed to a process of continuous improvement and, in years to come, would ideally like to achieve negligible water and raw material losses. Although the prospect of tightening legislation on effluent discharge had an influence, the driving force behind this initiative was simply good housekeeping, as the mill's Production Manager, John Gaunt explained, "If you run an efficient operation you have to recognise what you are throwing away. It is costing you money".

Scott Limited's tissue paper mill in Barrow-in-Furness in 1993 used on average 40% less water than it did in 1990. Just over half of this reduction was achieved by installing a dissolved air flotation plant that removes the majority of waste tissue fibres from effluent. This enables **recycling** of waste water back into the paper-making process. Flotation plants are particularly suited to the paper and tissue industry, but they can also be used in sewage and other industrial water treatment plants of all sizes.

In 1988 suspended solids in the mill's effluent were approaching NRA consent levels. Martin Kybert, Scott's Environmental Affairs Manager, says, "We were faced with two options. One was spending £1 million on a filtration plant that would have allowed us to keep just within current consent levels. Alternatively £2 million could be spent on a flotation plant and new filter screens which would allow us to stay well ahead of the game and enable us to recover and re-use significantly more fibre and water. It made sense to invest in the latter. We expect the plant to have paid for itself in about five years. It is staggering to think that so much money had been going down the drain in the form of waste fibre and water".

"It is staggering to think that so much money has been going down the drain in the form of waste fibre and water"

The remaining water savings have been achieved within the mill itself. A campaign was launched to make staff aware of the costs of wasting water. Ash Soni, Site Technical Leader, says, "Water is an expensive commodity and we use large quantities. Consumption was continuously monitored in the mill, but the campaign focussed our minds and we began to pay more attention to the data. We know how much water we should be using. Any discrepancies are reported in our daily production meetings, and action is taken promptly". The mill has also made a number of investments in more water efficient equipment, all of which have paid for themselves within a year. Pumps that require substantially less cooling water have been installed. The high pressure showers used to clean the fibre carrying belt have been replaced with some of a better design which not only clean more effectively but use less water. Ash Soni is confident that there is still room for cost effective improvement and hopes to reduce consumption by a further 10%.

3. WASTE REDUCTION

Waste Reduction CASE STUDIES

Introduction

Waste of materials means waste of money. The case histories in this section show how easily waste can be identified, once a process of monitoring is put in place, and how simple and cost effective many of the solutions turn out to be.

One leading waste consultant thinks that waste minimisation fails to get the attention it deserves because companies tend to underestimate the costs of waste. Ian Harrison, from Orr & Boss, says, "Most companies' accounting systems hide the cost of waste because a certain amount of loss of materials is tolerated as standard 'allowances'. The key to reducing waste and its costs is measuring all the separate components of the waste stream, and understanding how and where they arise".

Waste minimisation experts often refer to a hierarchy of strategies: reduction, re-use and recycling. Waste reduction, i.e. elimination at source, should be the primary goal, with re-use and recycling as back-up strategies. This chapter gives examples of waste reduction initiatives, with re-use and recycling covered in Chapter 4. Chapter 5 covers packaging, reduction of which can involve all three strategies. It has been treated separately because it is an issue of major environmental concern, and one which may well be subject to legislation, either European or UK-based.

More Effective Resource Use by Simple Means

The environmental measures taken by **Triplex Safety Glass Ltd.** automotive glass makers (part of the Pilkington Group) have been driven largely by cost considerations. Cost reduction targets are set and then targets for waste reduction are set by teams specialising in particular areas. Cost/waste reduction targets vary from 2% to 50%. According to Roger Leeming, European Production Manager, "One of the problems with waste is that the people who produce it are not always aware of its full cost implications. It's often someone else's responsibility to dispose of it or buy in the raw materials. By involving the entire workforce in our cost reduction programme we are bridging that gap and have had very encouraging results. For example, one of our plants uses a very expensive stainless steel cloth to protect glass against damage during processing. The team there saved £6,133 in the 1993/94 financial year, 21% of the budget for that item, simply by cutting the cloth on the spiral - a method which allows you to cut more pieces side by side. They very nearly met the target of achieving a 25% saving over the year".

> "One of the problems with waste is that the people who produce it are not always aware of its full cost implications"

One of the findings of an environmental audit of the UK branches and specialist businesses of **National Westminster Bank Plc,** completed in 1991, revealed that staff preferred to verify data from computer print-outs rather than directly from computer screens, resulting in large amounts of waste paper. A print-out review has been conducted to identify areas where paper savings can be made, and staff are now being made aware that wastage can, in many cases, be reduced by moving away from paper-based information. "In an organisation in which many different types of print-out are produced, the opportunity must be taken regularly to review content with the aim of eliminating some information or even whole print-outs. When it is, you become aware of considerable cost and environmental benefits", says Tony Sampson, Manager of the Bank's Environmental Management Unit.

In 1992 a 36,000 page print-out was ceased, saving £42,000 in paper, printing and manpower costs, simply by relying on screen-based information. Other print-outs have been significantly reduced by removing duplicated information. The Bank estimates that by continuing to target unnecessary printing, in this area of its business alone, savings of over £3 million per year can be achieved.

For **Forte Plc** the decision to look at the use of CFC-propelled aerosols showed up enormous wastage in the supply of **cleaning materials** to the company. Forte's concern about CFCs started back in 1983, long before international agreements to phase them out. At that time, the company's entire £500,000 per year supply of housekeeping cleaning products came in aerosols, and it seemed that convenience and ease of use were the main reasons. However, on looking more closely, it became clear that the propellants invariably ran out before the cleaning product. Then by talking to the suppliers, it was discovered that 80% of the cost of the product was in the aerosol packaging and labelling - so Forte asked them to find other ways of supplying the cleaning materials. The first types of hand-operated air pumps tried did not work well, but Forte encouraged the suppliers to keep trying. By the end of that year, an effective re-fillable plastic bottle was in use. By the end of the second year the cost of housekeeping cleaning products had been halved, saving **£250,000 per year.**

Quality Drives Towards Waste Reduction

For many years the sock division of **Simpson Wright and Lowe,** a Coats Viyella subsidiary, relied on final inspection to remove non-perfect goods. This was proving to be wasteful. An analysis of the costs involved led the company to tackle the problems at source, resulting in year on year savings in materials and production costs in excess of £100,000. Wastage, in the form of goods which had to be scrapped has fallen by 11%. The number of imperfects, which can be resold as seconds, has fallen by approximately 50%.

Lee Stephens, Development Executive, says, "The first part of sock manufacture, knitting, is conducted in single units. 85% of all imperfections are caused in this operation. When the goods leave the production unit to be dyed and finished the small units are batched into larger units, and it's at this point that items lose their identity in terms of their original point of manufacture. When we used to check for imperfections after dyeing we would know that a problem had occurred on one of say twenty machines, but we would not know which one. Not only that but the lengthy dyeing process meant that a week would go by before faulty goods were found. So, if the problem had not been rectified in maintenance checks, it would mean that we had another week's worth of goods with the same imperfection in production". The company now checks for imperfection prior to batching, enabling culprit machines to be easily traced.

> *"The principles used here can be adapted to any problem in any business sector"*

Simpson Wright and Lowe's simple solution required no investment. Lee Stephens explains, "There are a number of operations prior to batching which require the staff to pick up the socks. Rather than employ additional inspection staff, our existing staff have been instructed to check for imperfections at the same time". According to Lee Stephens, the time added is "virtually nil". Problems are reported to a departmental manager who completes a form and sends it to the department from where the goods originated. This department is required to respond formally, detailing remedial action taken. This information is always fed back to the person who raised the alarm. Lee Stephens views this as crucial, "We did not do this to begin with and we found that staff did not see the need to alert their managers to problems as it was never evident to them that anything was being done". The reports can also be analysed for re-occurring problems and, if necessary, machines or components are replaced. Lee Stephens says, "The principles used here can be adapted to any problem in any business sector. After all it is no more than directed common sense".

Finding New Technologies and Techniques

BP Chemicals Limited has achieved a **saving of £100,000 per annum** on one site by re-fitting valves on pipelines carrying hydrocarbons with an **improved sealing** arrangement.

BP Chemicals has made a public commitment to reduce hydrocarbon emissions to air by 50% between 1990 and 1997. Emissions generally come from either vents or leaks, and research showed that more than half the leaks were typically from the packing on valve stems, mainly on high pressure hydrocarbon pipelines. In 1990 total emissions from BP Chemicals' operations worldwide amounted to 60,000 tonnes of hydrocarbons, of which some 6,000 tonnes came from leaks.

"...are aware of the benefits to the company in keeping ahead of legislation..."

In a rigorous high temperature and pressure testing programme funded jointly by potential valve packing suppliers and BP Chemicals, one supplier's graphite-based product was demonstrated to be far more effective than its competitors. Although costing 10 times as much as the existing asbestos packing, the potential savings outweighed the initial investment concerns.

On the first site where valve re-packing was carried out, valve leaks totalled 400 tonnes and the payback on the £25,000 retrofit was a mere 3 months.

If the new packing technology is applied across all BP Chemicals' European sites over a period of 4 years, as intended, the savings are projected as 3,000 tonnes of hydrocarbons a year. Furthermore, there will be substantial savings on replacement and maintenance costs. The net total benefit will be in the order of £1 million per year.

BP Chemicals is aware of the benefits to the company in keeping ahead of legislation, and is the first company worldwide to have carried out such a comprehensive research programme in this particular area. Legislation on the acceptable level of Volatile Organic Compounds emissions (see page 88) applies currently in the United States and BP Chemicals expects the UK and Europe to follow before too long. It has also taken the initiative in spreading the word to other companies in its sector, by holding a forum in May 1994 to present its findings. Clive Twiggins, Mechanical Engineer, says, "There is no commercial advantage in keeping the project to ourselves. But there are significant public relations advantages in telling others. We can publicly state that we are doing something about our emissions levels, and we get profile benefit that way".

As a corollary to this exercise BP Chemicals has reviewed its policy for the purchase of new valves (see page 67), encouraging environmental awareness up the supplier chain. The benefit to BP Chemicals' corporate image together with the substantial environmental and economic savings, make the valve re-packing programme an enormous success.

The **Esso Petroleum Company Ltd** is responsible for the storage and delivery of petroleum fuels for 20% of the UK market. Since 1987, the company has invested £5 million to reduce vapour emissions from eight of its largest distribution terminals. "Through recovering over 4 million litres of petroleum annually, it is estimated that this investment was repaid within 3 years of completion of the last unit in 1990", says Patrick Roberts, Esso's Environment Adviser. Esso is the first oil company to have introduced this concept in the UK, doing so, well in advance of a proposed EC directive on Volatile Organic Compounds emissions from petrol. In 1993 the company received a major commendation from the Business Commitment to the Environment Awards for its achievements in this area.

As petroleum products are volatile, vapour escapes to the atmosphere whenever they are loaded and unloaded. For Esso this applies primarily to motor petrol during handling at terminals and service stations. "In 1985 it was decided that our vapour losses were undesirable, both environmentally and financially. We were effectively losing our product to the atmosphere when it could have been captured and turned back into liquid gasoline", says Patrick Roberts. A study was undertaken to assess the potential to reduce losses in the first place and, where that was not possible, to capture vapours and convert them back into liquid product via a simple recovery unit.

Eight of Esso's terminals have been equipped with sealed links and units to recover vapour released during product receipt into tankage and the outward loading of road tankers. As a result over 80% of gasoline throughput is now subject to vapour recovery and it is estimated that vapour emissions from terminals have been reduced by at least 50%.

To reduce losses further, investment has enabled road tankers to be loaded from the bottom rather than the top. This minimises disturbance to the liquid in tankers, reducing vapour formation. In addition, vapour balancing systems are being installed at major service stations. These ensure that whilst underground service station tanks are being filled with petrol, the vapour displaced is piped back to the delivery tanker. When the tanker returns to the terminal for filling, this vapour is captured, passed through a recovery unit and the resultant liquid fed back into the terminal tank.

In future years, the proposed EC directive on VOCs from petrol will require similar systems to be installed at terminals and service stations. Esso plan to equip its four remaining terminals and the remainder of its service stations in line with this requirement.

> *"....vapour emissions from terminals have been reduced by at least 50%"*

Lambson Fine Chemicals Ltd has **reduced its effluent disposal costs by £90,000 per year** and reduced its air emissions through the installation of **cleaner technology**.

The company already had strict control over measured emissions (as opposed to unintended leaks) at one of its manufacturing plants. However, there was a problem with fugitive emissions of ethyl mercaptan, which has a sulphurous odour that can be detected at parts per billion. Lambson intended to increase plant output by more than 50% during 1992/3, but realised that modifications had to be made to its processes to avoid unacceptable increases in odours, which had already prompted several public complaints. In addition, the removal of the effluent by a waste disposal company was costing Lambson £140,000 per year. The company became involved in the Aire and Calder Project (see page 24), and as a result, decided to install an improved liquid scrubber system.

A liquid scrubber handling system removes the sulphurous odours from the gaseous effluent. The scrubber liquid is alkaline and if acidified to neutral it can increase odour problems. To overcome this the liquid is treated with an oxidising agent. When the liquors are now moved, for instance into a tanker to take them off-site, there are no odours emitted. Dr David Anderson, Technical Environmental Director, says, "The technology is very simple, but it is applied with a high level of control to prevent any part of the process from causing problems".

As a result of making these modifications, the cost of disposing of the effluent to a chemical treatment site has been reduced by £90,000 per year. In addition, the effluent is now acceptable to the local sewage works (licensed to take Special Waste). Previously it went to a licensed chemical treatment site and the additional cost saving from this is estimated to be £3,600 per year. At the same time that this has been achieved, production, as planned, has increased by 50%.

As part of the involvement in the Aire and Calder Project, a Waste and Environmental Management System was introduced which has assisted greatly in the monitoring and control of processes impacting on the environment. Other benefits resulting from this include an audit of waste generated throughout the site, which encouraged Lambson to examine this area of its operations and make a number of modifications to reduce the overall waste load. Also, as part of a phased programme of work, the company has now completely isolated its operations from the adjacent River Aire, avoiding any discharge of unmonitored materials.

David Anderson says, "The Aire and Calder Project has been a good forum in which we could learn better skills for managing our environmental impacts and be able to show people that we are an industry that can bring about improvements from the inside. It has helped to raise awareness at all levels in the company. Lambson now operates a continuous process of environmental improvements".

"...and be able to show people that we are an industry that can bring about improvements from the inside"

Skippingdale Paper Products Ltd's nappy absorption pads used to be cut with high pressure water jets which not only consumed large quantities of water but also dragged pulp fibres from the pad. The resultant water and fibre slurry was sent to landfill. By switching to moulding, instead of cutting, Skippingdale no longer needs the water jets. Slurry, which used to amount to 5 tonnes per day, is no longer produced, saving Skippingdale £20,000 per year in landfill costs. Minimising fibre wastage by redesigning nappies to eliminate unnecessary padding, and through the adoption of moulding techniques, has led to annual **savings of £800,000** on pulp costs. The moulding equipment paid for itself in one year.

Glaxochem Ltd, a subsidiary of Glaxo Holdings plc, has a pharmaceuticals factory which operates an active programme to reduce losses of VOCs from production processes. Losses have been significantly reduced (approximately 1,500 tonnes per annum) representing annual savings of approximately **£1 million**. This has required some capital investment but Glaxochem estimates that several of these capital projects have achieved a payback of less than 12 months.

In 1991 a multi-disciplinary project team was formed to identify and quantify solvent (or VOC) releases. The team then recommended suitable approaches to prevent or minimise losses. "This work was initiated in line with Glaxo's commitment to continuous improvement in all aspects of health, safety and environmental protection under the Chemical Industries Association's voluntary Responsible Care Programme. The aim was not only to achieve environmental improvements but also to provide benefits in terms of energy conservation, waste minimisation and financial savings", says Tony Sherrard, the Factory Manager. The programme has enabled the factory to make good progress towards the VOC emission reduction targets established to comply with IPC authorisations.

Solvent losses were reduced through numerous operational, process and maintenance improvements. For instance, any leakage of air into filtration or drying plants operating under vacuum or the excessive use of nitrogen gas (used to reduce the explosion risk) increases the likelihood of solvent loss to vents and exhaust. By correcting nitrogen usage rates, where excessive, and regularly checking for air leakages, solvent usage has been markedly reduced. In addition, where losses could not be reduced by other means, capture followed by solvent recovery in existing units was introduced to improve the degree of solvent re-use.

"the key to progress was the pivotal role played by the multidisciplinary project team..."

Condition-based maintenance (maintenance triggered by changes in plant performance rather than unacceptable performance or breakdown) has played an important role. For example, portable detectors are now used routinely to check for low level leakages. The team also identified some opportunities to eliminate solvent usage altogether. A direct drying method, for instance, was developed to eliminate solvent usage in the dehydration of an enzyme, saving approximately 300 tonnes of solvent annually. In addition, considerable energy savings were made. New recovery technology was incorporated during a plant expansion leading to further solvent savings.

Glaxochem highlights that the key to progress was the pivotal role played by the multidisciplinary project team and the participation of all factory staff in reducing spillages and reporting on leaks. Efforts will continue in these important areas to ensure that further reductions can be achieved.

BP Chemicals Limited anticipates significant benefits from a **new strategy to detect soil contamination** from chemical storage tank leakages, using a new technology. The initiative is a component of the BP Chemicals Groundwater Strategy. Possible legislation on soil contamination is currently under discussion in the UK, and the desire to be prepared for any resulting measures has been a major driving force behind the Strategy.

Aware of the need to assess the extent of soil contamination, BP developed a "diffuse monitor probe" for detecting hydrocarbon vapours in soil. The device consists of a hollow spike, 0.3 metres long, which is knocked into the ground. Inserted into the top is a tube containing a chemical sensitive to hydrocarbon vapours. The vapours enter through holes in the spike and are collected in the tube over a 24 hour period. The tube is then capped and sent away for analysis. The technique will be used mostly as an initial screening technique to discover potential trouble spots, from which soil and water samples can then be taken.

The technique has been used to pin-point successfully a leaking tank on one of BP Chemicals' sites. The company was aware of the possibility of some contamination on the site, resulting from the activities of the previous site owners, when standards of containment were much lower than they are today. However, employing the diffuse monitor probes in a grid pattern showed that there was actually a leak from a group of tanks, adding to the background contamination, a result BP Chemicals did not expect. Martyn Lambson, Soil and Groundwater Consultant, says, "It was clear that further work was required both to pin-point and to stop the leakage occurring. Also there is a value in the leaked material and if we can stop the leak, we can save money". BP Chemicals is now engaged in the follow-up work.

The other economic benefit to BP Chemicals is that the process allows the company to plan ahead in the long term management of a site. BP Chemicals believes that when it decides to sell a site, it will be confident that it has a full understanding of any problems with the ground and will have a better feel for the commercial value of the site and what it can do with it.

The clean-up process that will result from a better assessment of contaminated sites will be costly and, before the discovery of this ongoing leak, BP Chemicals was not anticipating any short term financial benefit from using the diffuse monitor probe process. Martyn Lambson explains the overall benefit to the business, "BP Chemicals Groundwater Strategy has allowed us to identify existing pollution, even when unexpected, and it allows us to target expenditure at the highest risk areas. So we are putting our money where it is needed".

4. RE-USE AND RECYCLING

Recycling

CASE STUDIES

Car Recycling

One definition of waste is materials for which there is no longer any use. However, many things are put into this category prematurely, without full consideration of the extent to which they could be re-used, given the right conditions. Environmental policy makers will increasingly look to "close the loop" of raw materials use, production and waste - in other words, to make sure that as little goes into production cycles, and as little comes out, as possible. The following case histories demonstrate imaginative approaches to "closing the loop", whether this is within an individual plant, or within a group of companies. The principle remains the same - what was once considered waste, becomes a valuable raw material.

Car Recycling

ACORD, the Automotive Consortium on Recycling and Disposal, is an example of cross-sector co-operation in the establishment of environmentally beneficial disposal methods, with representatives from all the major UK vehicle manufacturers, trade associations, the disposal industry and Government. ACORD's proposed target for old cars (known in the trade as "end of life vehicles") is to send only 15% of a car's weight to landfill by 2002 and to reduce this figure to 5% by 2015. The current figure is 23%.

The group has put together a Preliminary Operating Plan to develop facilities and legislation to improve recycling. 98% of metals are currently re-used, but there are difficulties in recycling non-metallic car parts (which constitute 30% of a car's weight), particularly plastics, and many materials cannot at present be recycled economically. ACORD encourages manufacturers to improve the recyclability of their products and improve the market for recycled materials within the motor industry. In addition, Government is urged to investigate taxation policy as a means of encouraging the use of recycled material and discouraging landfill, and to support recycling technology and market creation projects.

A major driver to ACORD's efforts is a recognition of the importance of contributing to the European Community Priority Waste Stream project "End of Life Vehicles", instigated by The European Commission, on behalf of British industry. This cross-sector co-operation demonstrates the potential for achieving significant advances in assuming responsibility for much of the product life-cycle, from manufacturing to disposal.

Recycling of Process Waste

Like many foundries, **Alfer Limited** (part of the Baxi Partnership Limited) had a problem with dust from the process of making the moulds for casting metal parts for domestic heating equipment and other components. In the normal sand moulding process, dust is produced and has to be extracted from the air to keep the working environment in the foundry in good condition. Once extracted and passed through a "wet scrubber" the result was a dirty sludge which had to be transported by road and dumped in landfill. David Sumner, the Project Engineer at Baxi, started to think about eliminating this sludge for a combination of reasons: the cost of dumping, the irritation to local residents by spillage from the lorries and, not least, the fact that the sludge still contained quantities of clay which was itself an expensive commodity. The answer was a pumping system that re-introduced the sludge to the mould-making process and which was developed in 1983 for a foundry that has since been replaced. The same system was installed in a foundry opened in 1988 to produce a new range of castings, where all the sludge, approximately 1,300 cubic metres a year, is recycled to make new moulds. **Savings on clay and disposal costs are estimated to be between £40,000 and £50,000 per year** after taking into account costs for cleaning the wet scrubber. The capital outlay of £19,000 was recouped within four months. As a result of this achievement Baxi was awarded both the British and European Better Environment Awards for Industry in 1988.

> *"The capital outlay of £19,000 was recouped within 4 months"*

By operating a **"closed loop" recycling system** for plastic off-cuts, **Nissan Motor Manufacturing (UK) Limited** (NMUK) saved, in 1993, in excess of **£700,000** on raw materials. Capital investment in machinery was recouped within 15 months.

On all Micra and Primera cars NMUK has introduced high density polyethylene (HDPE) fuel tanks that incorporate a nylon layer to reduce fuel vapour loss through the plastic. NMUK was the first to develop this to meet the requirements of certain European countries. During tank manufacture the production of significant quantities of off-cuts, amounting to approximately 30-40% of the total weight of each tank, is unavoidable. High density polyethylene contaminated with nylon used to be considered unsuitable for re-using in the original product as nylon aggregates caused imperfections. Off-cuts were therefore sent to landfill.

Concern about the sheer quantities wasted and the cost of landfill led an NMUK engineer to develop the technology which now enables all off-cuts to be re-used. The off-cuts are granulated and then pelletised before being fed back into the process. The granulation achieves nylon particles of a sufficiently small size to mix uniformly the nylon and virgin HDPE, overcoming the problem of imperfections. Tanks currently comprise 40% recycled material. Studies are in progress to assess the potential to increase this to 60%, allowing all damaged tanks to be recycled, without compromising the integrity of the tank.

It is NMUK's policy to improve environmental performance at no net cost to the business and, therefore, ultimately the customer. Dr Les Nicholls, Director of Engineering and Chairman of the Environmental Planning Group, says, "Our policy allows me to incur costs to achieve environmental objectives, provided as a minimum I am generating other initiatives which save at least the same amount of money. I can therefore pay for environmental initiatives that will never pay for themselves. It is not hard to generate ideas which cost money and this policy imposes a vigilance on us to be watching constantly for initiatives that will save money". The plastic off-cut recycling paid for a switch to water-based paints on the Micra car, which in turn helped to reduce solvent emissions.

The plastics recovery initiative is also a product of NMUK policy to place accountability and responsibility at the most appropriate point in the company. Les Nicholls comments, "Traditionally an engineer has little or no management or financial accountability, but with this project an engineer had total accountability. He had the detailed knowledge of the process, he knew what to test for in order to attempt to address the wastage problem. Only he could set feasible targets. He took responsibility for the job and in the end solving the problem was his own achievement".

The automotive glass makers **Triplex Safety Glass Ltd.** (part of the Pilkington Group) benefits to the tune of **£273,890 a year** simply by **segregating waste glass** and thereby greatly enhancing its recycling potential.

Roger Leeming, European Production Manager, says, "All glass waste used to go into the same skip and we paid £53,890 a year to send it to landfill. Segregating it has made it a useful resource for a company that now pays us £220,000 a year to take it away. It's a win-win situation". Untreated glass waste is recycled to make patterned and wired glass products. A market has now been identified for scrap laminated, toughened and printed glass, all of which were previously landfilled. This "contaminated glass" is now used as an aggregate in cement and as a reflective material in road marking paint.

Moves towards quality management have also helped change the culture of the company. Triplex has the BS 5750 standard for quality and, although it does not address the issue of waste directly, according to Derek Norman, Pilkington's Director of Environmental Affairs, "As you take the 5750 culture through, you start to think about waste and regard it not as waste, but as somebody else's raw material".

"As you take the 5750 culture through, you start to think about waste and regard it not as waste, but as somebody else's raw material"

Similarly, by **segregating paper waste** from general waste and selling it for recycling, the Triplex plant has saved **£756** on landfill charges over the period of one year. A team of staff are setting targets to minimise paper consumption as part of the cost reduction programme (see page 31). Posters by photocopying machines remind staff to utilise double-side photocopying facilities wherever possible and efforts are now being focussed on eliminating unnecessary computer print-outs (National Westminster Bank case study - see page 31).

By taking a **fresh approach to waste management**, Gerald Buckingham, Waste Co-ordinator for **Standard Products Ltd UK**, reduced waste disposal costs from **£30,000 per month to £5,000 per month in six months**, without any capital costs at all.

The Standard Products plant in Plymouth, which manufactures rubber door and window seals for the UK, European and North American car industry, used to send approximately 50 containers measuring 35 cubic yards to landfill every month. This waste amounted to about 20% of the company's raw materials. Gerald Buckingham devised a simple plan to reduce this, starting with the separation of the waste products. Some were suitable for immediate recycling, such as the waste rubber compound, which is sold for re-use in carpet backing, floor insulation and playground surfaces, and now brings in up to £50 per tonne for the company.

"Getting waste costs down to about £5,000 a month from about £30,000 took us from April 1991 until October 1991. Apart from the rubber, we were selling pallets and getting money back for paper. These all became incomes, to the tune of about £3,000; so at the end of this, waste disposal in fact cost us about £2,000 net."

A more difficult challenge is that posed by the waste "profiles" of rubber compound moulded on to steel or stainless steel and aluminium. However, by taking the concept of separation one step further, Standard Products, in conjunction with a firm in Scotland, are now able to recycle all materials in these waste products. A granulator is used to grind down the material, which is then passed through a magnetic field to remove the steel, and a "densimetric table", which measures the density of the different components, to shake out the aluminium. All parts of the "profile" are therefore separated and able to be re-used as "clean" products, bringing in savings of approximately £4,850 per week.

By applying similar principles to plastics, a branch of the business which had not been operating to its full capability is now making a greater profit. 20% of the PVC bought was wasted and sent to landfill before a buyer was found. The company could only get £10 per tonne for the PVC, most of which had an aluminium strip fixed to it, making it difficult to recycle. Gerald Buckingham devised a method for removing the strip and was then able to sell the PVC for £60 per tonne. The company is working on re-introducing the recycled PVC back into its processes at a proportion of 15-20%, thereby reducing the quantity of virgin material needed. The company predicts possible savings of £270,000 per year from these measures.

The latest project for Standard Products is to reclaim the rubber compound to the standard required to mix it with virgin material for the making of new car parts, leading to 100% elimination of waste on this particular stream. The company anticipates that this will be achieved in conjunction with a Dutch rubber recycling company, with assistance from the Department of Trade and Industry through the EUREKA programme (See page 82). The company believes, "This reclaiming process, if successfully introduced and implemented, will save many thousands of pounds, not only for Standard Products, but also for other companies working with this type of rubber compound throughout the world. And just as important is the fact that less waste is being disposed of, saving acres of land from being filled with virtually indestructible waste".

Gerald Buckingham acknowledges that there are problems with addressing waste management, "You are trying to meet deadlines and targets and you have to have the quality right for your customer. If you increase the quality, you have to be careful not to increase the waste. You have to start off with a will to succeed and the thought processes to see it through. It is not a question of black and white, but trial and error. Success is often achieved by simply trying something and finding it works".

"Success is often achieved by simply trying something and finding it works"

Recycling of Post Consumer Waste

Stricter waste disposal controls and higher landfill costs have led **BMW (GB) Ltd** to find ecologically and financially sound disposal routes for products previously thought of as waste.

In December 1992, in a joint initiative, BMW and Bolney Motors, a company with 13 years experience of marketing used car parts, established a **car recycling plant** with the capacity to handle two and a half thousand scrapped cars per year. By recycling, the weight of landfill waste from each vehicle is reduced by an average of 46%. As the process develops, BMW believes the remaining waste can be reduced by more than half again. In 1993 Bolney Motors processed 610 cars at its plant. In the same year BMW received the Automobile Association's Environmental Concern Award for setting up the plant.

Each vehicle is dismantled in a way that achieves maximum economy. High value components, such as gear boxes, starter motors, pumps and electronic parts are re-conditioned and re-sold, ferrous metals are returned for shredding at steel mills at £35 per tonne and aluminium is forwarded to a smelter at a value of £600 per tonne. Some rubber, plastic and glass materials are returned to the raw materials suppliers for between £50 and £380 per tonne. Some materials which BMW cannot yet recycle are used for generating energy, and the remaining inorganic and inert materials are sent to landfill. In 1993 BMW recovered 100,000 gallons of oil and 30,000 lead acid batteries, and the company is planning to start shortly the recovery of waste brake fluid which will be recycled into new BMW standard brake fluid.

The main difficulties have been the establishment of recycling routes for plastic and rubber materials. BMW has teamed up with other car manufacturers to find ways of avoiding landfill disposal for plastics. Current initiatives focus on the recycling of components which are either sorted, granulated and remoulded into new products, or repaired and re-conditioned. The company says, "Every time a perfectly re-usable component is employed instead of a brand new one, the cost of producing that component in the factory is avoided". Where possible, plastic materials used in making new BMW cars are chosen specifically for their ability to be recycled. For example, plastic bumpers are currently recycled into components such as boot linings for the BMW 3 Series.

> *"Whilst vehicle recycling within the UK is still in its infancy, there is already commercial value for the materials so preventing them ending up in landfill"*

The project is still very much in its infancy and total savings have not yet been calculated. At present, it is still cheaper to dispose of some items to landfill, but, based on the company's experience in Germany, Carl Sanderson, Service Project Manager for BMW, believes that once an infrastructure is established for recycled materials, "it is likely that profitability will be realised within two-three years", allowing eventually for lower prices for the consumer.

The plant is intended to be "a commercial business rather than a pilot or demonstration plant", and is the first of a network of 15 sites around the country to be developed by 1995. "Whilst vehicle recycling within the UK is still in its infancy, there is already commercial value for the materials so preventing them ending up in landfill."

Matsushita Electric UK Ltd anticipates saving **£100,000 per year** by 1995 on its waste disposal costs, having achieved **100% recyclability** of its expanded polystyrene packaging material.

Matsushita estimates that by 1995 the volume of its expanded polystyrene waste, used to protect televisions and microwave ovens, will have reached 57,500 cubic metres. Expanded polystyrene is slow to biodegrade so landfill sites are reluctant to accept it; it cannot be incinerated because it gives rise to toxic fumes; and because it is bulky and light, it is uneconomical for potential users to transport.

During the 1980s the expanded polystyrene was re-used for cavity wall insulation, but with the decline in the construction industry, the market shrank and a viable alternative had to be found. Furthermore, "1992 environmental legislation which includes Duty of Care and Cradle to Grave provisions (see page 87), have meant that Matsushita Electric (UK) Ltd has had to examine its methods of waste disposal even more thoroughly". (Quote from a MEL UK Environmental Report).

The system adopted involves the compaction of the material by 47:1 using machinery paid for by Flopak Ltd, who then transports it for re-processing at its plant. Flopak recycles the polystyrene back to crystal polystyrene to produce new packaging with commercial benefit to itself. In 1992 Matsushita received the Golden Leaf Award for Responsible Environment Management in Wales in recognition of its work in this area.

Matsushita says, "By adopting this method of disposal, we have solved our environmental problem of disposal and storage, eliminated our transport costs and effectively closed the loop by achievement of 100% recycled product". Cost savings from reduced transport plus a small amount of revenue from the compacted waste came to approximately £60,000 in 1992 and are projected to rise to £100,000 by

1995. And, despite the fact that Flopak is still having to transport the material, the compaction means 47 times fewer journeys.

*"By adopting this method...
we have solved our environmental
problem of disposal and storage,
eliminated our transport costs and
effectively closed the loop by achievement
of 100% recycled product"*

Since the company installed this system, it has made presentations on behalf of the Welsh Development Agency to users and producers of expanded polystyrene in South Wales. Its example is also now being adopted by other companies in the same sector and it is hoped that a smaller version of Matsushita's system will become available for the use of retail outlets and fast food chains which have a high polystyrene usage. Matsushita's responsible approach to waste management, and its success, has encouraged it to talk to its polystyrene supplier with a view to "commencing a project to investigate 100% re-use of the crystal polystyrene produced by this method". It believes that the system is readily transferable and that, if other companies using such material follow its example, it will have "solved a worldwide environmental problem".

British Polythene Industries plc made the decision to undertake an ambitious recycling programme as a result of increased environmental awareness and anticipation of European legislation on "cradle to grave" responsibility for products and packaging.

Anaplast Ltd, one of the group's companies, manufactures polythene packaging in the form of sacks and products for agricultural and building use. Agriculture has moved towards using more products that are either contained in plastic packaging or that are made of plastic, such as silage wrap and crop covers. This has caused a disposal problem for farmers. Farmers used to burn this material, but that became illegal after the 1989 revision of the Clean Air Act. The remaining options were for the farmer to bury the material on his own land, which is not practical because polythene does not biodegrade, or to send it to landfill, which is costly.

BPI decided to take responsibility for the disposal of its own products and put in place a subsidiary company called Second Life Plastics, to collect waste polythene from farms through a network of 32 regional agents in the UK. The polythene is baled and sent for recycling, where it is shredded and then put through four or five washing and reduction processes and ultimately pelletised. Anaplast stores the pellets in silos until required for use in a new product. The recycled material can be used in various proportions with virgin material or can be used on its own, mainly for lower grade agricultural polythenes, such as pit liners. In 1992 Anaplast received a Golden Leaf Award for its recycling programme.

Anaplast produces about 7,700 tonnes of agricultural film a year and in 1993, Second Life Plastics collected and recycled in excess of 4,500 tonnes, a significant percentage of the original product.

At the time the scheme was conceived, Anaplast believed it made financial sense, that it would be cheaper to collect and recycle than it would be to purchase prime polymer. But because of the swings of the commodities market, an excess capacity in the production of polymer has currently forced the price down. It is possible to go from making money to losing money many times in a year, so although Anaplast is buying less raw material, the company is currently losing money from this activity.

The company therefore approached other manufacturers and suppliers of agricultural polythene to establish whether they were willing to bear part of the cost of running Second Life Plastics, in proportion to their output. The outcome has been a series of meetings between Government and representatives from across the industry. A draft plan has been devised whereby Second Life Plastics will be taken over by the plastics industry as a whole and funded by all companies that supply polythene to agriculture.

"Our industry uses a non-renewable resource as a feedstock and we all have to be involved in conserving that stock. That is what sustainability, as far as we are concerned, is all about"

Andrew Heatherington, Environment Manager, says, "It would make sense to transfer this initiative to the industry, in order that not only the cost, but the benefits of the scheme can be equally spread. Our industry uses a non-renewable resource as a feedstock and we all have to be involved in conserving that stock. That is what sustainability, as far as we are concerned, is all about. The long term viability of our industry as a whole will be more secure if an even higher proportion of this material can be returned to the manufacturing process, resulting in less virgin material being used, as well as assisting farmers with a difficult disposal burden".

Ricoh UK Products Ltd has developed unique processes and manufacturing procedures in the production of selenium coated aluminium photocopier drums. During the period April 1989 to March 1992, these developments **reduced drum manufacture costs by 54%**. This enabled Ricoh to lower the average price of photocopiers by 25%. In 1993 the company received a Queen's Award for Environmental Achievement in recognition of its work in this area.

A number of concerns led to the initiation of what became known as the "drum production improvement project". Manufacture originally involved using CFCs and it was the policy of the parent company to eliminate CFCs from all production facilities by the end of 1993, almost four years ahead of international legislation. In addition, the consumption of raw materials - namely selenium, aluminium and solvents - was seen to be too high and did not take advantage of the potential for recycling. Also photocopier drums require replacement throughout the life of a copy machine. As selenium is extremely toxic it has been Ricoh's policy to take back used drums to ensure their safe disposal. Over the years a large stockpile of drums, which were either used products or rejects from the manufacturing process, had built up and was awaiting disposal.

A team of technologists and engineers at Ricoh's Telford site were given the task of addressing these concerns. A key objective was to create a closed system in which all selenium and aluminium waste, whether from the production process or returned products, would be re-used either by Ricoh, in drum production, or in the products of other manufacturers. This objective has since been achieved.

To eliminate CFCs, which were used to clean tubes after coating with selenium, a new method of high pressure water cleaning was introduced. This also reduced a lengthy solvent degreasing process, the result being that solvent consumption in this process fell by 75%. Another problem in the production process was the high grade selenium waste generated during drum coating. Through improving the method of its collection and through working with the supplier, it has been made possible for Ricoh to use a new selenium alloy which incorporates all of this waste.

Prior to disposal, the stockpile of used and rejected drums would require processing to remove the selenium coating. Under the conventional method selenium recovery and the re-use of aluminium tubes was not possible. However, a new method was developed by the project team which enables all of the selenium to be recovered and returned to the supplier for re-processing so that it can be incorporated into the selenium alloy used by Ricoh and used again in other products. The new method also means that aluminium drums that have a sufficiently good surface finish after selenium removal can be re-used by Ricoh, and now account for 30% of drums used in their production process. Damaged drums are returned to the supplier and, through collaborating with them, the technical specification of the alloy used to make new drums has been changed, allowing it to include 30% of the returned aluminium. The remaining 70% is recycled for use in other products. Waste stockpiles have now been eliminated.

Combined with improvements in the efficiency of materials' utilisation - for instance, the efficiency of coating drums with selenium has almost doubled - overall consumption of selenium and aluminium has been reduced by 70% and 39% respectively. The various elements of the project were phased in over three years, ending in 1992, during which time the drum manufacture department maintained full production.

John Dutton, First Manufacturing Manager, says, "It is difficult to calculate the exact rate of return on the total investment of £342,900, as the cost savings have been passed on to the customer in order to maintain a commercial position in an increasingly competitive marketplace. However, it is possible to attribute cost savings arising from reduced materials consumption. This would suggest a payback period of 9 months".

Recycling

Waste

5. PACKAGING

Packaging CASE STUDIES

If industries do not succeed with waste reduction and re-use on their own, measures may be forced on them by legislation. Each year Britain's packaging industry consumes 1.6 million tonnes of glass, 1 million tonnes of plastic, 2.4 million tonnes of paper and board and 800,000 tonnes of steel and aluminium. The European Union is currently considering a Directive on packaging which would place responsibility for disposal of packaging waste firmly on the producers. Policy makers are also likely to want to influence the choice of disposal options. In most of Continental Europe, and to some extent in the UK, sending waste to landfill is considered a wasteful use of land. Levies are under consideration to make landfill relatively more expensive than other options such as incineration and recycling.

Producer Responsibility Industry Group

According to the UK Government's Sustainable Development Strategy it wanted industries involved in the packaging chain to prepare a plan for introducing producer responsibility for packaging, which was to include:

- the need for an effective organisation, spanning all the relevant business sectors, which can both prepare and implement the plan;
- commitment by industry that it will meet the costs necessary to fund new collection and processing capacity and the creation of a mechanism for raising the necessary finances;
- a staged plan building up progressively to overall recovery levels of between 50-75% by 2000, but recognising the scope to expand collection and processing capacity within the next year;
- a willingness by industry to increase demand for recycled material where it meets appropriate standards;
- immediate action to safeguard the recycling infrastructure for plastics and paper and board threatened by subsidised German imports.

In February 1994 the Producer Responsibility Industry Group presented "Real Value from Packaging Waste - A Way Forward" to the Secretary of State for the Environment and the President of the Board of Trade.

Two further reports have been published which deal with comments received on the orginal report and one specifically which deals with the levy to fund the PRG plan.

Reducing and Re-using Transit Packaging

Nissan Motor Manufacturing (UK) Ltd (NMUK) claims that no other
European car company is as far advanced, in volume terms, with re-usable
packaging. NMUK receives from Japan engine blocks, gearboxes and small parts,
i.e. nuts, bolts and washers, for their Micra and Primera cars. The UK and the rest
of Europe supply all other components. Through liaising closely with suppliers and
hauliers, NMUK now receives 96% of European components in packaging which is
returned to the supplier for re-use. This figure is expected to rise to 98% in 1996.
Returnable packaging consists of polythene boxes and frames or "stillages" into
which fit movable shelves uniquely designed to hold a supplier's components.
Shelves are replaced or modernised as and when components change. Standardised
stillages and boxes are aimed at making best use of space during transit as well as
storage and improved handling.

In 1987 all component packaging waste was either sent to landfill or incinerated.
Frank Charlton, Materials Handling Manager, says, "At that time 90% of our
supplies arrived in disposable packaging, which we had to throw away. In 1990 a
cardboard baler was installed to compact and bale cardboard which was then sold
for recycling. It paid for itself in 2 years but it was a false economy. We were getting
money back from something that was a waste product when really what we needed
to do was eliminate the waste at source".

> *"We were getting money back from something that was a waste product when really what we needed to do was eliminate the waste at source"*

The costs of investing in returnable component packaging are offset by the
immediate savings made on landfill and incineration costs and over the longer term
by the reduction in the costs of the packaging itself. Payback on capital investment
made by NMUK varies from supplier to supplier, but is often under a year and
always less than two.

Once returnable packaging on a particular component has paid for itself, annual
savings are earmarked for investment in environmental initiatives which will not pay
for themselves. This is in accordance with NMUK environmental policy to improve
environmental performance at no overall net cost to the business (see also page 38).
"It is difficult to calculate overall savings achieved to date as when Micra
production commenced in 1992 a number of suppliers started on re-usable
packaging straight away, so we had nothing to compare it with. However with one
UK supplier an investment of £4,500 was repaid within 2 months in reduced
material costs alone, amounting to overall savings of approximately £27,000 in
1993", says Frank Charlton.

In 1993 NMUK won an RSA Environmental Management Award for "making the
Nissan Micra responsibly". The use of returnable packaging and the recycling of
petrol tank off-cuts (see page 38) were among the achievements highlighted.

Bluecrest Convenience Foods Limited a supplier of chilled and frozen meals to
the major supermarkets, has recently initiated a project which it believes will **save a
substantial proportion of its packaging costs.**

The company has, until recently, packaged its products in corrugated cardboard
cases for transportation but, with customers' agreement, it is now moving towards a
policy of shrink-wrapping products direct on to pallets. This not only saves on
packing materials but, it is anticipated, will produce savings in transportation costs
due to more efficient use of space in delivery vehicles.

The only outlay required is for the equipment to carry out the shrink-wrapping,
which costs approximately £17,000. It is too early to estimate the cost benefits that
will accrue from this as the new method was only put into operation in March
1994, but the environmental benefits are explained by Richard Hallett, Production
Director, "The shrink wrap is recyclable, and instead of having the problems
associated with recycling weighty and bulky cardboard, it is much more
compressible, and more easily put back into the recycling chain". The new method

will also produce a benefit to the customer, who will not have to dispose of or return so much waste.

Ambler of Ballyclare, a yarn spinning subsidiary company of Coats Viyella, has saved **£16-18,000 a year** on materials as a result of eliminating the use of polythene bags in yarn packaging. No investment was required, quality was not adversely affected nor were there adverse reactions from customers. 35,000 bags used to be consumed weekly to protect the yarn from soiling in transit. Yarn is now packed in boxes, but without the outer polythene wrapping, and more care is taken to protect it from dirt in transit. Mike Lawford, Environmental Co-ordinator of Coats Viyella, says, "Reproducing this principle across other Group production units, will mean substantial cost and raw material savings. Communication of this initiative throughout the Group has led to other successful packaging reduction initiatives". Ambler now also uses re-usable cartons when distributing products to certain customers. These are flat-packed and sent back to the depot once emptied. Cartons used to be disposed of after each use, but the re-usable ones have a life of at least four years, with only cardboard sleeves having to be replaced after this time - the plastic tops and bottoms do not deteriorate. This realises annual savings of approximately £10,000.

> *"We had to ask ourselves what would happen in a few years time when people will not want packaging and when responsibility for packaging disposal shifts onto the manufacturer"*

These initiatives were taken in accordance with Group environmental policy to minimise wastage and cost. Peter White, Chairman of the Group Environmental Management steering group, comments, "We had to ask ourselves what would happen in a few years time when people will not want packaging and when responsibility for packaging disposal shifts on to the manufacturer".

The initiatives stemmed from multi-disciplinary project teams in each Coats Viyella company, set up to examine packaging needs, and involving staff with varied expertise and responsibility. Such teams have been found to generate fresh approaches and enthusiasm. Peter White says, "Ownership of projects at grass roots level is crucial. Responsibility for the environment is focused on the people on the ground who are creating the waste, on a day-to-day basis. They have to be conscious that their actions produce results".

> *"Responsibility for the environment is focussed on the people on the ground who are creating the waste, on a day-to-day basis. They have to be conscious that their actions produce results"*

Another illustration of this approach is in the Homewares Division of **Coats Viyella Plc** which has identified savings of **£100,000** a year to be made on the packaging used to transport materials between sites. Again no capital investment is required. Savings will be achieved by reducing the gauge of polythene and cardboard packaging and by using recycled instead of virgin polythene.

For Coats Viyella a logical extension of its successful efforts to reduce inter-site packaging would be to look at reducing, or even eliminating, the packaging on finished products, subject to customer and quality requirements.

A Comprehensive Packaging Audit

Concern about packaging is not new to **Boots The Chemists Ltd** where, for 20 years, long-life returnable crates and metal roll cages have been used to deliver products from warehouses to stores. The alternative would have been to consume millions of cardboard boxes each year. In 1992 the company won a major commendation in the Business Commitment to the Environment Awards for re-using the plastic trays in which sandwiches are delivered and displayed. Trays now make four trips instead of one, saving 200 tonnes of plastic annually.

Building on these successes, in 1993 Boots carried out a comprehensive **packaging audit**. The audit was aimed at meeting the company's 1991 commitment to minimise the environmental impact of packaging without compromising the needs of safety, product protection and consumer information. The audit established the types, content and quantities of all retail, display and transit packaging, covering all 50,000 lines handled by the company. Boots then set targets for the reduction, re-use and recycling of packaging materials. The primary motivation for conducting the audit was environmental improvement, which Boots says forms an integral part of its ethical approach to business. At the same time the company has made savings in the order of thousands of pounds. In May 1994 the Boots packaging audit was commended by the RSA Environmental Management Award Scheme.

> *"The audit was aimed at meeting the company's 1991 commitment to minimise the environmental impact of packaging without compromising the needs of safety, product protection and consumer information"*

The audit was the result of an 18 month development and trial period and involved product managers, technologists and warehouse staff. Product managers visited warehouses to review packaging usage. "This proved to be a real eye-opener, raising the awareness of the total amounts involved, 70,000 tonnes of packaging material in 1993 alone", says Belinda Howell, Environmental Project Manager. Suppliers were asked to provide a breakdown of the type and level of materials used, together with information on recycled content and re-use rates, with sample verifications of this data done by Boots staff.

As a result of the audit over 70 tonnes of paper/board and 180 tonnes of plastic were saved and 27 tonnes of virgin pulp have been replaced by recycled fibre. According to Belinda Howell, "We calculate that packaging reductions alone have saved in excess of 14,000 giga joules of energy and almost 230 cubic metres of solid waste".

> *"Actions resulting from the audit come under the three target categories of reduce, re-use and recycle"*

Actions resulting from the audit come under the three target categories of reduce, re-use and recycle. They include an 88% *reduction*, by weight, in the packaging of Boots Terry Nappies by switching from a box to a polythene pack with a recycled paper label. Boots is currently extending to all stores the *re-use* of plastic transit and display packaging for Boots No 7 powder compacts. On average five trips are now being made instead of one. Boots believe that using *recycled* materials helps to create a market for them and in 1993 launched product ranges with retail packaging made from recycled materials including first aid, toys and batteries. The drive to use recycled materials where available, so long as they are of adequate quality and value for money, continues in all areas of Boots' operations. In addition, Boots identify the materials used in plastic containers which will assist with recycling sorting as schemes are introduced.

Using Refills to Reduce Packaging

Procter & Gamble Limited is achieving **significant savings in packaging materials** for powder and liquid washing detergents through the introduction of a **refill concept**. The benefit is passed on to the customer as a price reduction.

Procter & Gamble has had an environmental policy for over 25 years. At the end of the 1980s the company decided to update this and coined the phrase "more from less" to describe its approach to looking at the environmental impacts of its products.

In 1990 the company reformulated Ariel detergent to produce a more concentrated product, using 30% less ingredients by changing the product formula, but achieving results as good if not better. Since its introduction, 300,000 tonnes of ingredients have been saved. This has also given a reduction of 30%, or 30,000 tonnes, in the product packaging required and thus a substantial reduction in costs.

Procter & Gamble saw further opportunities to reduce packaging by selling its liquid and powder detergents in refill containers. The pouch used for the liquid detergent uses 70% less packaging material than the normal plastic bottle and the company estimates that over 11,000 tonnes of packaging material have been saved as a result of these refills over a 4 year period. For the powder detergent Procter & Gamble introduced a plastic laminated refill container which uses 90% less material by weight than the traditional cardboard carton. These packs have to be transported in stronger cases, so the overall saving on powder detergent packaging is around 50%.

Countering possible criticism over the move to plastic, Procter & Gamble says that its refill bag has equivalent environmental impact to other refill packaging options but offers consumers and the trade a more robust container.

David Hammond, Environmental Affairs Manager, says, "We very quickly changed consumer habits because we offered a reduced price of around 20p for a refill pack, so we have passed much of the savings on to the customer. That was a key part to getting the idea up and running". Liquid refills now account for 80-90% of the overall liquid detergent market, as other producers have followed Procter & Gamble into the refill market.

> *"...we have passed much of the savings on to the customer"*

> *"We see a three win situation in this sort of initiative: the consumer wins because they get better results, the environment wins because we are using less material and it is good for business..."*

The company uses recycled materials in its packaging wherever possible and pioneered the use of post-consumer recycled plastic in bottles. In co-operation with suppliers, the technology was developed to produce a bottle with virgin plastic on the inside and outside of the bottle, with a layer of post-consumer waste in between - the "sandwich" bottle. The recycled material will constitute 50% of the container when the technology is fully developed. Currently this process is more expensive than producing bottles with purely virgin material, but David Hammond says, "We have seen it as part of our investment in encouraging the recycling industry, in order to get it started in this country. The potential is there for it to become economically viable and contribute to a sustainable business". As part of this, Procter & Gamble is involved in a local scheme in Sussex to collect post-consumer household plastics.

The company believes that the whole philosophy of "more from less", which is applied throughout the business, keeps it ahead in a very competitive industry. David Hammond says, "We see a three win situation in this sort of initiative: the consumer wins because they get better results, the environment wins because we are using less material and it is good for business - we have seen a substantial part of the market move to this so we are obviously addressing a consumer concern".

6. REDUCING THE IMPACT OF TRANSPORT

Transport CASE STUDIES

In 1990 the Government estimated that traffic in the UK would increase between 83 and 142% by the year 2025. These projections were welcomed by some as a sign of growth.

Since that time we have become increasingly aware of the environmental impacts of transport. Transport is responsible for around 24% of CO_2 emissions in the UK, and the proportion is growing. Local air quality is affected by emissions of nitrogen oxides, carbon monoxide, smoke and the chemicals that lead to low-level ozone. There is increasing evidence that sensitivity to asthma and other respiratory complaints is linked to traffic pollution, and the benefits of catalytic converters in reducing emissions will be quickly overtaken by sheer traffic growth. Congested roads not only slow down business, but generate even more pollution, and building more roads tends to lead simply to more traffic. The continual demand for land on which to build roads has meant a growing catalogue of damage to Sites of Special Scientific Interest (SSSIs - see page 88) and other valued natural areas.

The Government now acknowledges that unlimited traffic growth will have unacceptable consequences for the environment. The debate has only just started on how to reconcile the needs of companies and private travellers with a more environmentally-friendly transport policy, but companies can already make important contributions to limiting environmental impacts. They can take steps to reduce the number of vehicle miles travelled in the course of their business. Proven measures include consolidating loads, compacting products and waste in order to use less vehicle space, and either eliminating packaging, or switching to more space-efficient forms. They can also use cars with smaller and more efficient engines, choose cars with the most up to date pollution abatement technology and train their drivers to drive responsibly. There is also the possibility of minimising wastage through recycling in-house, using re-usable packaging or eliminating packaging altogether. All of these can lead to reduced demand for vehicles to take waste for disposal. The case studies below illustrate a number of these approaches.

Driving

Driving for Efficiency

In 1993 **DHL International (UK) Ltd** delivered 80 million packages to 70,000 destinations in 218 countries. Transport is, therefore, the company's main environmental concern. As issues of traffic congestion and pollutants from fuels move steadily up the public and political agenda it is likely to remain DHL's main concern.

As part of an environmental Action Plan, DHL has set itself the task of improving fuel efficiency by 15% by mid-1996. Such a target represents a real challenge for a company that drives, on average, 15 million miles each year in the UK, consuming 2½ million litres of fuel. According to Katharine Robinson, Environment Manager, "Meeting this target will mean an estimated saving of £358,000 over the next three years, literally making our fuel and our money go further, and benefiting the environment".

"if you can't monitor it, you can't manage it"

Encouraged by studies that have shown that the way a vehicle is driven can affect fuel consumption by up to 20%, DHL has established a **Fuel Efficiency Driving Scheme** for all its drivers, including the Directors. The two key concepts are communication and monitoring - "if you can't monitor it, you can't manage it". Records of fuel consumption are maintained for each driver and where performance is not meeting targets, action is taken in the form of vehicle servicing or extra driver training. The careful choice of the most fuel-efficient vehicles for each operation also makes a contribution to meeting targets. At the same time, regular route planning ensures that the most efficient routes are used on all journeys.

Another initiative is DHL's "Team Buses". Instead of individual courier vans, DHL has begun to use "Team Buses" for journeys from the Heathrow depot to central London. Couriers sort the consignments on the buses en route and deliver the goods on foot. This has so far reduced the number of vans travelling in and out of London per day from 18 to 2 and speeded up customer service and delivery times, which is good for business.

Strong management commitment is important for the success of the programme. Quality and Environment have been brought together within the senior management team, to ensure the continued drive for improvements from the highest level. Katharine Robinson is working with managers and staff in all parts of the company to implement new initiatives and explore their ideas for improvement.

Staff understanding and motivation is also essential to the success of DHL's fuel efficient driving scheme. This has been achieved by issuing the handbook "In Gear for a Better Environment" to all staff. This explains the simple precautions everyone can take to reduce the environmental impact of driving a vehicle. Also important is the fuel efficiency league table
of departments and depots. This has the effect of motivating staff because nobody likes to be at the bottom of the league.

> *"...environmental sense really is commercial sense"*

According to Katharine Robinson, "The idea behind our scheme is not new. It's the combination of commitment, monitoring, reporting, communication, route planning, vehicle selection and driver training that is different. This combination has enabled us to harness the enthusiasm of all our managers and drivers - to improve their driving skills, save money and improve the environment. Because, as we've demonstrated, environmental sense really is commercial sense".

More Compact Goods Means Less Transport

Through compaction and improved design **Skippingdale Paper Products Ltd** has reduced the volume of disposable nappy packs by almost 60%, saving **£195,000 per year** in transportation costs in the UK and to Scandinavia. Lorry loads have been reduced to such an extent that approximately 600,000 km less are travelled per year. New compaction packaging equipment, designed by Skippingdale, paid for itself in 6 months. Since introducing compaction the major brands in the UK have been following Skippingdale's example. Skippingdale is currently redesigning its equipment to achieve even further compaction, and it is hoped that volumes will be reduced by a further 20%.

Volumes have also been reduced by redesigning and moulding the nappies to eliminate unnecessary padding, ensuring that thickness of the pad varies according to where it is most needed. This, in combination with the use of super-absorbent materials has reduced the weight of a nappy from 70g to 55g. Skippingdale hopes that with further work on design it will be possible to reduce the weight to 45g.

> *"... not only do we save on transportation costs ourselves, but our customers also make savings"*

Skippingdale supplies major retailers with nappies packaged as their own brands. 25% of its nappies are exported to Scandinavian retailers, the remainder to retailers throughout the UK. It was the high cost of transporting to Scandinavian retailers that prompted the Managing Director, Mats Akesson, and his Sales Manager to investigate how to increase the number of nappy packs per lorry.

There are knock-on benefits for Skippingdale's customers, as Mats Akesson explains, "We deliver to depots from where our customers distribute to their individual shops. So not only do we save on transportation costs ourselves, but our customers also make savings".

Procter & Gamble Limited has saved in the region of **16,500 lorry journeys** between 1990 and 1993 by producing a more compact product and cutting down on packaging.

The company has operated an environmental policy for over 25 years, but increasing consumer concern over environmental issues towards the end of the 1980s led Procter & Gamble to re-examine all the environmental impacts of its products. By developing a new technology for Ariel detergent, the company has been able to reduce by 30% per wash the quantity of product needed to achieve results as good as, or better than, traditional detergents, with related reductions in packaging. In addition, the introduction of refill packs has also contributed to a reduction in the use of packaging materials (see page 49).

By achieving this, the company are able to fit more packs on each lorry, requiring fewer journeys. David Hammond, Environmental Affairs Manager, says, "The most important area to look at when reducing output to the environment is product use. If the product gives better performance using fewer ingredients and less material, that feeds right back up the production process to less packaging, raw materials and transport". Significant reductions in distribution costs mean less fuel consumption, fewer vehicles, reduced emissions and a positive contribution to decreasing congestion on supply routes. At present, compact detergents account for around 50% of the total detergent market. Procter & Gamble is looking to secure the remaining 50%, doubling the benefits already achieved in reduced transport costs and impacts.

> *"Without taking a long term view one may fail to recognise that within a potential environmental benefit there can also be a financial benefit"*

The **National Westminster Bank Plc** has been recycling waste paper for many years. An environmental audit of the Bank's UK branches and specialist businesses, completed in 1991, highlighted the fact that paper was disposed of uncompacted. By installing paper waste compacters in approximately 1,850 of its branches, the Bank has **halved the number of journeys** that need to be made by waste contractor vehicles and space required for interim storage has been reduced. In some branches it also reduced the need to make otherwise necessary conversion work on storage areas to meet fire regulations.

The Bank estimates that the compacters will provide an estimated financial advantage of £640,000 over a five year period. This figure takes into account investment made, payback and inflation. "Without taking a long term view one may fail to recognise that within a potential environmental benefit, in real terms, there can also be a financial benefit", says Tony Sampson, Manager of the Bank's Environmental Management Unit.

Better Technology

TNT Express (U.K.) Limited is saving 12-17% of its annual fuel used by applying research into **vehicle design and specification and fitting aerodynamic devices**.

TNT began researching ways of reducing costs and improving service in the mid-1980s as the business diversified from mainly parcels delivery to contract distribution of goods for clients across a range of businesses with very different needs.

The company's engineers developed computer models which included operating costs, weight calculation for vehicle stability and engine performance, to increase understanding of the basics of the efficient delivery vehicle. At the same time, they began looking into the possibility of applying aerodynamic components to vehicles as a means of fine-tuning the basic design. By 1989-90 TNT was achieving good initial results in terms of fuel economy, performance and positive driver feedback on vehicle stability and noise reduction.

These achievements were noticed by the Department of Energy. In 1991 the Energy Technology Support Unit (ETSU - see page 81) offered to provide funding and facilities for further research. As part of the agreement, after completion of the work, TNT personnel travelled round the country with Department of Energy representatives to talk to operators in all road transport sectors about the possible benefits that could be realised as a result of their work.

The outcome of TNT's research is that the company now operates vehicles that give a greatly improved overall performance. By taking into account different types of loads and weight, the basic vehicle is adjusted to enhance stability and the most appropriate engine, gearbox and rear axle combination. A three-dimensional aerodynamic device is fitted to the cab, front corners of the bodyworks are rounded, side skirts fitted between the front and rear axles and the rear roof scooped. All these devices further enhance stability and driver control and reduce air drag.

> "...you can become more competitive... more efficient, more reliable and you can reduce the number of vehicles you have on the road "

The cost of adapting a tractor unit/semi-trailer combination vehicle in 1991 was £3,000. Fuel savings amount to £3,500 per year (on 1991 fuel costs) on a vehicle travelling in excess of 100,000 miles per year, so the payback is less than one year. TNT operates 370 such vehicles in its commercial fleet of 2,669. For the smaller, rigid delivery vehicles the technology is scaled down; the payback is slightly longer on these vehicles as the mileage covered is normally less, but average fuel savings are still at least 12-13%. For a similar fleet, without any of the adaptations implemented by TNT, an annual fuel bill would be in the region of £20 million. TNT is saving £2.5 million on this figure.

In addition to fuel savings, and the accompanying reductions in emissions of oxides of nitrogen (NO_x), CO_2 and other pollutants, there are other benefits that are harder to quantify, but which are also significant. These include increased stability, reduced road noise, reduced spray and improved trip times, through better driveability and sustained high average speeds, which ensures the vehicle is being driven at maximum fuel efficiency speed. As a result of TNT's involvement in spreading the word about its work, many companies have asked its advice. Alan Parker, Director of Engineering, says, "Here was an operator who had achieved results and could tell others about the benefits. We did not only want to win on this one - we wanted to pass the benefits around and now there are lots of other large companies mirroring our vehicle designs".

Alan Parker believes it is important to underline that the benefits to any business in undertaking such initiatives are very wide, "Your operation can benefit, you can become more competitive in the market, you can become more efficient, more reliable and you can reduce the number of vehicles you have on the road".

Technology

7. NEW BUSINESS OPPORTUNITIES AND IMPROVED COMPETITIVENESS

Competitiveness

Environmental initiatives can lead to increased market share and opportunities for new products because the public is increasingly sensitive to environmental issues. According to the head of the polling organisation MORI, nearly half the British public say that they have selected one product over another because of its environmentally-friendly packaging, formulation or advertising. Although it is always very difficult firmly to attribute changes in market share to one particular factor, the companies we have featured here are convinced that environmental responsibility has improved their business. Savings achieved through waste reduction, re-use and recycling can help to keep prices low in highly competitive market places and can also enable companies to maintain or increase market share.

We have been able to include only a few examples of new products here, but the opportunities implied by these examples are considerable. As discussed in the chapter on waste, the pressures to find new uses for materials previously considered waste are growing all the time, and the only added ingredient needed is imagination. There is also continual demand for new, cleaner technologies to meet regulatory demands as well as to improve the efficiency of industrial processes.

Business Opportunities from New Technology

For **Elm Energy & Recycling (UK) Limited**, environmental concerns have meant a major new business opportunity. The company will **provide energy by burning scrap tyres**, and intends to burn up to 20% of tyres scrapped in the UK. The project is designed to meet several environmental objectives at once: reducing the number of tyres going to landfill; saving on the use of fossil fuel resources; and producing a fraction of the pollutants emitted by conventional coal or oil fired power stations.

Burning tyres produces more British Thermal Units (BTUs) per pound than high grade coals and the company claims that it takes just two tyres to meet an average home's daily electricity requirements. Elm Energy avoids the problem of air pollution by installing a unique scrubbing and air clean-up system.

> "...it takes just two tyres to meet an average home's daily electricity requirements"

The high temperatures generated by the tyre burning process that was specified by Elm ensures that any dioxins are eliminated. Each furnace is designed with a series of "Pulse Hearths" which progressively shovel the burning tyre materials through each stage of the heat/steam generating process. The most valuable by-product, steel wire, is collected and transported off-site for recycling by the metals industry.

At separate stages in the process, the flue gases are filtered. In the final stage, virtually all particulate matter, which is principally zinc oxide, is removed and also sent for recycling. At optimum operating conditions, 15,000 tonnes of steel wire and 2,300 tonnes of zinc oxide will be extracted for re-sale. At the final stage further processing of the flue gases ensures that they meet the most demanding HMIP conditions, after which they are emitted via a stack to the atmosphere.

The project has received support and encouragement from various Government departments, and is subsidised under the Non-Fossil Fuel Obligation's Renewable Energy Programme (see page 88). It is also a long term disposal alternative that complies with the "Duty of Care" provisions in the Environmental Protection Act 1990.

Commercial viability of the scheme, which has only been operating since October 1993, is assured by charging for waste tyre disposal, the sale of electricity to Midlands Electricity Plc and the materials recycled from the burning process. All the major tyre manufacturers have already signed contracts with Elm Energy. Scrap tyres remain a real environmental problem, but Elm is providing an answer that not only benefits the tyre industry, but is also an innovative business opportunity.

Edwards High Vacuum International (part of The BOC Group plc) identified **new markets** for a technology developed to deal with a problem specific to the electronics industry. As a result, in 1993, the company won a Queen's Award for Environmental Achievement for making a significant contribution to reducing pollution in the chemical industry.

In the electronics industry vacuum pumps are used to create a vacuum in the electronic chip manufacturing process. The oil used to seal the vacuum pumps became contaminated with process vapours, and could also migrate back into the vacuum chamber, causing contamination in the process. The industry was therefore looking for an oil-free pump. In response, and after much research and development effort, Edwards developed a "dry pump". The patented Edwards mechanism relies on designing and machining parts precisely. The size of the gap between moving parts is reduced so far that there is no need for sealing.

Taking the thinking a step further, Edwards engineers were familiar with a different kind of problem being experienced with oil and water sealed pumps in the chemical and pharmaceutical industries. Here pumps are used primarily to create a vacuum during distillation and drying processes. Vapours from the process which passed through the pump would come into contact with the sealant and contaminate it. Edwards estimate that worldwide these traditional types of pumps generate daily in the order of 1 million tonnes of contaminated effluent, leading to a costly treatment and disposal problem. "By removing the need for oil and water sealants, dry vacuum pumps can eliminate that effluent at source", says John Skeates, Chemical Sector Business Manager. "In addition, solvents passing through 'wet' pumps themselves become contaminated with the seal fluid. Such contamination does not occur with dry pumps making solvent recovery or treatment much simpler." The first Edwards pump was installed in a chemical plant in 1987.

> *"We see ourselves as world leaders in dry vacuum pump technology. We have more pumps in the field than any other manufacturer"*

"We see ourselves as world leaders in dry vacuum pump technology. We have more pumps in the field than any other manufacturer. We hope this is going to be a growing business and will provide jobs and profit for the company for years to come", says John Skeates. "Indeed, HMIP authorisations are forcing companies in the UK to pay particular attention to the effluent from vacuum systems. We see the dry pump as being the solution." In 1994 dry vacuum systems were recommended as a best available technique under the Oslo and Paris conventions on the Prevention of Marine Pollution.

In 1986, 45% of world consumption of CFC 113 was used by the electronics industry for printed circuit board cleaning. 1986 is the base year for the CFC reduction calculations of the international Montreal Protocol for the protection of the ozone layer. Nitrogen inerted soldering, pioneered in the UK by **BOC Gases Europe**, provides the electronics industry with technology that eliminates CFC usage and contaminated aqueous effluents from printed circuit board manufacture. Not only that, it also saves its customers money. According to Market Development Manager, Colin Precious, BOC **leads the market in the UK**, where it believes nitrogen inerted soldering will become the industry standard.

Conventional soldering in circuit board production uses a tin-lead alloy solder, with a resin flux or paste to combat the formation of oxides on metal surfaces during processing. Soldering usually results in a corrosive residue which has to be removed, often using CFC solvents. This is to prevent circuit failures when the boards are in service. The alternative is to wash off the residue using aqueous based or semi-aqueous cleaning, but this results in the formation of effluent (contaminated with metal salts) which is costly to dispose of. Another disadvantage of such systems is that a considerable amount of energy is consumed when the boards are subsequently rinsed and dried.

In 1987, with the lack of satisfactory alternative cleaning systems and international legislation to phase out CFCs looming, research was concentrated on producing an atmosphere in which to perform soldering with minimal residue production. The result was a nitrogen based atmosphere, "Nitraclean", which was used with a paste to leave virtually no residue following soldering. Since 1991, BOC's efforts have centred on promoting its second generation "Nitraclean" atmospheres. These work with all the new generations of low residue fluxes and pastes.

"...it also saves its customers money"

"The best solution is to eliminate the need for cleaning in the first place", says Colin Precious. "Soldering under nitrogen means that you do not have to prevent oxide formation during processing and it also improves solderability. Therefore you no longer need the traditional high solids content fluxes which leave a residue that usually needs to be cleaned off. "Nitraclean" used in combination with low solid (or no-clean) fluxes/pastes allows post-solder cleaning to be completely eliminated. The phase-out of CFC cleaners has a clear environmental benefit because less damage is done to the ozone layer. Avoiding aqueous or semi-aqueous cleaning reduces the energy requirements of the process and eliminates the effluent stream disposal costs."

Machine purchase costs are higher for nitrogen-capable equipment (which is sealed to minimise gas escape) and a nitrogen atmosphere has a cost, whereas air is free. However, according to BOC, payback can be achieved in less than a year. Savings will be made on CFCs, or on the water, energy and disposal costs associated with aqueous cleaning methods. In wave soldering, a large amount of "dross" (lead and tin oxides that float on the molten solder) is formed when operating in air and significant amounts of solder are lost in removing it. Dross formation is virtually eliminated in a nitrogen atmosphere resulting in a substantial reduction in solder consumption and associated maintenance.

Environmental concerns have moved on from CFCs to the use of leaded solders and fluxes containing Volatile Organic Compounds (VOCs). Because nitrogen helps maintain good solderability at the higher temperatures required by lead free solders and aqueous fluxes, the industry is likely to be steered further towards inerted soldering.

Environmental group **Greenpeace International Ltd** has created a new product opportunity for refrigerator manufacturers by demonstrating that there are viable alternatives to using environmentally-damaging chemicals in domestic fridges.

The CFCs used as coolants in fridges contribute to depletion of the Earth's ozone layer, and their production and use is due to be phased out over the next few years under the international agreement known as the Montreal Protocol. However, Greenpeace became concerned that CFCs would be replaced by a new generation of similar chemicals, HCFCs and HFCs. HCFCs still deplete ozone and HFCs are potent global warming gases which face controls under the International Climate Convention. Greenpeace set out to prove that environmentally acceptable, cost effective and technically-proven alternatives should be used instead.

Greenpeace in the UK commissioned the first prototype fridge using hydrocarbon (propane and butane) coolants from London South Bank University in 1992. These hydrocarbons are non-toxic, have no impact on the ozone layer and virtually no impact on global warming. After the UK work, the technology got off the ground in Germany where a manufacturer was quickly found. In 1992 the German office of Greenpeace was in discussion with technicians from the Dortmund Institute of Hygiene who were developing a fridge using hydrocarbon coolants, and with expanded polystyrene for insulation rather than CFC-blown foam. Greenpeace then commissioned DKK Scharfenstein, a fridge manufacturer in former East Germany, to develop a series of prototypes. The coolants worked well, and the fridges were shown not to have higher energy consumption than conventional models, a point put by other German manufacturers as one of the reasons for not adopting hydrocarbon technology.

In mid-1992 work on the fridge was in danger of being stopped when the company was threatened with liquidation. Greenpeace successfully argued for Sharfenstein's survival, and generated nearly 100,000 advance orders through a large mailshot. Greenpeace also secured support and start-up funding from the German Ministry of Environment. Full scale production started in March 1993, and the "Greenfreeze" fridge now carries the German "Blue Angel" eco-label.

As from 1994, all the major German manufacturers have announced that they will produce only hydrocarbon fridges. Bosch-Siemens and Leibherr have stated that they will convert nearly all of their production to "Greenfreeze" technology by 1995, and AEG have just announced the same target. "Greenfreeze" also has the market advantage of now being more energy efficient than most other fridges available. Corin Millais, Ozone Campaigner for Greenpeace UK, says, "In 1992 all these manufacturers were strategically committed to environmentally damaging HFCs and HCFCs. German manufacturers have shown that protecting the environment makes good business sense". At present, no British company is manufacturing and selling hydrocarbon fridges in the UK. Electrolux is making "Greenfreeze" fridges in the UK for the German market, but UK consumers have to buy imported German models. Greenpeace campaigners are hoping that this situation will change.

Greenpeace acknowledges that by making the switch now, German manufacturers may simply be pre-empting future controls of HFCs (under the Climate Convention) and HCFCs (under the Montreal Protocol). Taking up the technology so quickly shows that they are confident of a strong market for environmental goods, and of securing competitive advantage by being seen to act early in the interests of the environment.

Business Opportunities from Recycling

Acme United Limited has opened up a profitable market by **developing a new product made purely from recycled materials**. Its nail scissors, made of recycled plastic and steel, have taken over 8% of the UK market, worth **£3 million**, and the introduction of a range of recycled kitchen knives and scissors has increased sales by 10% or £300,000. In 1994 Acme's kitchen scissors were voted Environmental Product of the Year by the industry journal "DIY Week".

The idea came from Acme's parent company in the USA which had used polystyrene from fast food containers for the manufacture of scissors. Acme United in Sheffield decided to adopt and improve on this concept. At this time, one of Acme's existing buyers, Boots The Chemists, was establishing its credentials as an environmentally concerned company, and signalled a willingness to support the idea. Such encouragement from a large buyer was very important.

"Such encouragement from a large buyer was very important"

Through undertaking market research, Acme established that one important factor in consumer decisions was the protection of the environment. Steve Foster, of Marketing Direction, consultants to Acme, comments, "Buyers do take the opportunities if they are there. The choice of an environmentally improved product had not been there before. The consumer has no problem with the idea that recycling is a logical, realistic and responsible thing to be doing. He or she is constantly faced with publicity about it". Acme also had to be aware of consumer concerns about quality and price in order to reach as wide a market as possible.

Discussions with The Body Shop International plc established a buyer for recycled nail scissors and other cosmetic items, such as tweezers, and also provided Acme with a reliable supplier of post-consumer plastic from the Body Shop bottle tops. Boots, already a buyer of kitchen knives and scissors from Acme, now stocks the recycled range, under the Boots brand name. The potential here is considerable as Boots has 30% of the market for these products. Other smaller contracts are under negotiation.

Virtually all the company's production is now involved in recycling. Growing awareness within the company of environmental concerns has led to a belief in the necessity for a wider view. "Most environmental products depend on niche marketing, but the whole point about environmental concerns is that they are global and have to be to succeed. Acme is aiming at the global arena as its niche. Recycled knives and scissors could be sold to everybody", says Steve Foster.

Paper Back Limited, a small company **selling recycled paper products**, has shown that there is a market for goods that consumers perceive to have a less-damaging impact on the environment. In the ten years since the company was set up, it has achieved a turnover of £3 million per annum and now employs 26 staff.

In the early 1980s there were very few recycled paper products available. Those that did reach the market were not high quality and there were frequent customer complaints. Market research demonstrated that a market for recycled papers existed, so Paper Back approached the Paper Industry Research Association (PIRA) and, with assistance from a Government grant, carried out extensive research into improving the quality of recycled paper. The outcome was a new product launched in 1985-6, the first matt-coated recycled paper and which was, according to Jan Kuiper, Business Development Manager, "a breakthrough in terms of quality".

Paper Back's products are, on the whole, at least 50% genuine post-consumer waste (paper that has been used as opposed to mill or printers' off-cuts) and the environmental benefits are numerous. The most obvious benefit is that recycling means less overall waste creation and less of a disposal problem. The UK still disposes of more than 6 million tonnes of waste paper every year, most of which is dumped in landfill sites. Over the last 5 years Paper Back has sold recycled paper equivalent to over 10,000 tonnes of waste paper. In addition, recycled paper consumes 50% less energy than paper products made from virgin pulp, giving less CO_2 emissions, less water use and a reduced disposal burden. Jan Kuiper says, "Collected waste paper is virtually ready to be made into a new product. It just needs to be put into a hydro-pulper and cleaned, which is mainly done mechanically rather than chemically. You are therefore leaving out several steps in the paper-making process when you make your product from waste paper". These steps include the application of fertiliser to grow the trees, the energy consumed in the felling and logging processes and the use of water in the pulping and transportation, usually from abroad.

> *"Until 1989 we doubled our turnover every year"*

Despite early difficulties in developing and marketing a suitable product, Paper Back was seeing a return on its initial investment in its second year of trading. Jan Kuiper, who is also one of the founders of the company, says, "We didn't expect the growth we actually experienced in the 1980s when we started. Until 1989 we doubled our turnover every year. The recession and a substantial drop in new paper prices slowed our rate of growth but we are now looking forward to growth in the rest of the 1990s".

Paper Back now sells a whole range of recycled paper products and has also diversified into supplying office accessories, which promote the potential for using products made from more durable materials or with a higher waste content. As technology develops further, the company hopes to expand the range of papers it offers.

> *"Although there has always been a strong ethical underpinning of the company, we also believed there were clear economic benefits - the intention was to make a business out of it and ensure we were financially successful in the market"*

The company has proved that there is a sustainable market for its products. Jan Kuiper says, "Although there has always been a strong ethical underpinning of the company, we also believed there were clear economic benefits - the intention was to make a business out of it and ensure we were financially successful in the market". His view is that if you believe in your products and you have the enthusiasm and marketing skills, then, "Have a go! The socio-political climate works in our favour as we have to tackle environmental problems - we cannot get away from them because the Earth has limited resources".

Improved Competitiveness Through Better Environmental Performance

Aware of increasing consumer demand for products which have a less-damaging impact on the environment, **Wade Furniture Ltd** has taken a number of steps which John Warburton, Commercial Director, believes have given the company **"a tremendous marketing edge"**.

Wishing to offer customers a choice and promote environmental awareness, the company has developed a range of yew furniture in which all the solid woods and linings, as well as the temperate soft wood yew veneers, come from regions other than tropical rainforests. Developing this range entailed a high risk factor as John Warburton explains, "We can buy a tropical timber in the veneer form for about 60p a square metre, yet I can't buy any temperate hardwood for anything below £1.20 per square metre. We have launched a product on the market that is, pound for pound, more expensive". However, Wade found that consumers were enthusiastic about the yew range, which has now become a major part of its business.

> *"...we are just ordinary furniture people trying to be responsible because we are using a product which is sensitive".*

An important move for the company has been to switch to the use of veneers as opposed to solid woods. Before 1989 Wade had a tradition of building everything in solid timber, mainly mahogany and oak. Apart from giving more flexibility in the types of timber that can be used, veneering is an excellent conservation technique; one cubic metre of timber would produce 40 square metres of one-inch thick timber, but the same cubic metre would produce 1,666 square metres of veneer. By using veneers, Wade is able to maximise its use of sensitive timbers, whilst using carefully selected timbers and particle board for the backing boards and solid wood sections. Following an audit by botanist Sara Oldfield and conservationist John Burton, the company has phased out its use of endangered species such as rosewood and is constantly exploring alternatives to the tropical timbers it has been using. In 1993 Wade won an RSA Environmental Management Award for promoting the reality of sustainable tropical timber.

As part of the company's commitment to protecting the environment, Wade is supporting the Programme for Belize. The organisation is committed to protecting tropical forest in Belize, as well as exploring the best ways of selectively logging high value trees without damaging water courses, understanding how forests regenerate, developing a model for husbanding techniques and building a code of good practice that can be applied to other parts of the world. John Warburton explains, "Our long term aim is that we should solve the problem not just for Wade Furniture, but for everyone. We are not environmental experts ... we are just ordinary furniture people trying to be responsible because we are using a product which is sensitive". From a purely commercial point of view, the company wants to achieve a reliable source - it needs mahogany and other species to be around in future years, otherwise it will not have a business to run.

Wade has a policy of informing its customers of its approach to environmental management, which includes tickets on each item of furniture, and catalogues and booklets for traders and the public, which have a company statement about the sustainability of the timbers used and informs people of the Programme for Belize. It is this dissemination of information that Wade believes has had an impact on its recent sales, although it is impossible to estimate the extent of that impact. John Warburton says, "Over the last few years we have had growth on growth each year during a recession, a very deep recession as far as furniture is concerned. Obviously one of the reasons is that we are making a product that people want, but I don't think that is the full story. I believe much of it is down to the environmental initiative".

In 1991 **Boots The Chemists Ltd** was the first to introduce lightweight refills for canisters of its own brand baby wipes, saving 39 tonnes of plastic a year. Melanie Lidiard-Phillips, Product Manager, states, "Within six months we had increased our market share and become the clear market leader in this area. We can confidently say that this was as a direct result of introducing the refill packs".

B&Q plc has explicitly acknowledged the market advantages of good environmental performance, "B&Q firmly believes that a business which is efficient, which complies with or exceeds all environmental legislation, which is innovative in finding less damaging products and which is respected by opinion-formers will be a business which meets the demands of its customers and inspires the confidence of its investors".

As a result of introducing a comprehensive supplier environmental audit into its buying process, it is B&Q's intention to offer the consumer products which come from an environmentally and socially less destructive source. Its policy on peat is one example. Peat extraction often damages areas designated as Sites of Special Scientific Interest (SSSIs - see page 78) so B&Q now offers a range of peat alternatives and ensures that the peat it does sell does not originate from SSSIs. Sales of alternatives now account for 35% of sales in this product area, demonstrating the scale of customer concern and the potential for business advantage. The company was awarded the 1992 Premier Award for Business Commitment to the Environment in recognition of its policy on peat.

In 1993, one of the company's stores ran a display of energy efficient products in Energy Efficiency Week to coincide with the Government's media campaign on energy use. Sales of products such as energy efficient light bulbs increased by 93%, which shows the potential gains from effective marketing strategies of "greener" products.

The company is not claiming to offer a range of "green" products as such; it is bringing environmental concerns to all the products which it stocks. Dr Alan Knight says, "We see the environment more as a customer service, which of course, has a sales advantage. What we want is for people to say they will shop at B&Q because they believe we are good on the environment and sort out which products are good and which are not".

A year after launching its Ethical Policy in May 1992 **The Co-operative Bank plc** increased its retail deposits by 13% and profits for 1992 were up by £16 million. At the end of 1993 retail deposits rose a further 16% and profits rose another £8 million. The Bank believes that the policy and performance are strongly connected.

After carrying out a comprehensive programme of market research amongst Co-operative Bank customers and non-customers, the Bank drew up a draft policy which it circulated to 30,000 of its customers, both personal and business. Customers were asked to indicate their level of concern about the ethical issues in the draft. The individual issues which were incorporated into the final policy statement were all supported by an average of 79% of those polled. 84% of them believed in the positive value of an ethical policy.

More than 70% of customers polled in 1991 believed the Bank should include issues of environmental pollution, exploitation of scarce resources, energy conservation, use of recycled materials and support for environmental organisations in its policy. The policy applies both to the Bank's financial services for business customers and the provision of investment services to tax-exempt bodies, such as pension funds and charities. These institutions have the choice of investing in the Co-operative Bank Ethical Unit Trust which was introduced in 1993 after the Bank's Ethical Policy was developed. It currently has £11.5 million under management. The Bank employs the Ethical Investment Research Service (EIRIS) to look at the top 500 quoted companies and recommend where the bank should invest by applying the criteria adopted by its ethical fund, which mirrors the Bank's Ethical Policy.

The Bank is confident that it can offer a range of ethical banking products and services to its customers. In a recent advertisement, the bank states, "Our customers know there are some things we will never invest in, such as companies whose activities are needlessly harmful to the environment". Where customers are concerned, the policy states, "[The Co-operative Bank] will encourage business customers to take a pro-active stance on the environmental impact of their own activities".

"Merely expressing concern, however, is not enough. We believe that we should do all we can to promote action for a better environment"

The Bank is keen to take a positive approach, and uses its "voice" as a means of encouraging environmentally sensitive practices. The Bank receives regular advice from a number of environmental organisations, many of which are themselves customers of the Bank. Chris Smith, Group Public Affairs Manager, says, "It's not always a case of 'comply with our ethical policy or go'. We are becoming much more alert to the role of adviser in these matters and call upon external expert advice to pass on to our customers".

However, "voice" may work sometimes, but "exit" is the only route if that fails. When the policy was launched 5 business customers were asked to leave the bank and more than 40 have been refused as new customers for ethical reasons. One of the bank's publicity booklets states, "We are aware that all industry, transport and farming can cause damage. We appreciate that the world's resources are by no means limitless. Merely expressing concern, however, is not enough. We believe that we should do all we can to promote action for a better environment." The response, particularly from small- and medium-sized enterprises (SMEs), who constitute the majority of the Co-operative Bank's customers, has been very favourable. Chris Smith says, "All companies, including ourselves, need help and advice at some stage on these issues. With regular newsletters and personal visits we are now helping companies of all sizes put ethics and environmental issues on the agenda". In a new initiative, a scheme has been set up with the Groundwork Trust (see page 79) to provide a free consultation on environmental matters for customers.

"I am delighted that our ethical stance has struck a chord both with our customers and potential customers"

By promoting a strong ethical stance the Bank gives customers and potential customers the chance to decide whether the Co-operative Bank deserves their support. It has taken the risk of offending some, but drawing support and business from others. The bank has turned a £6 million loss in January 1992 to a profit of £17.8 million in January 1994 during a period when the major banks were suffering financially.

Terry Thomas, Managing Director, says, "I am delighted that our ethical stance has struck a chord both with our customers and potential customers".

The UK retail battery market is dominated by two leading companies, and **Varta Ltd** is the third brand. At the end of 1993 the company claimed 9.3% volume share of the total battery market, a share which, according to Varta, has grown annually by a minimum of 10% since 1989. Varta attributes its market position to the innovative way in which it has approached the market and to a succession of environmental initiatives where it has claims to have been "first and fastest past the post". In 1990 Varta received a Green Award for Marketing and the Environment from the Worshipful Company of Marketers.

The most recent initiative was in May 1994, when Varta was the first to launch a branded range of Alkaline and Zinc Chloride batteries in plastic-free blister packs. The packs are 100% recyclable, being made only of cardboard. The cardboard itself is made of 80-90% recycled fibres. Graphics on the front of the card give the impression that it is a normal blister pack, thereby retaining, in Varta's view, maximum impact at the point of sale.

"Because of the widely recognised benefits of our environmental initiatives, we normally have about a six month window of opportunity before other manufacturers follow our lead, and we expect this will be true for our new blister-packs. However, we believe there is always a prize for being first", says Paul Fildes, Varta's UK Marketing Manager. "Amongst retailers packaging is a prime concern, and this is one reason why we feel our new all card blister-packs will be welcomed, as indeed our other initiatives have been. We think consumers will respond favourably too, especially given that, in a 1993 INFOPLAN survey, their two key concerns were identified as being CFCs and packaging."

8. LOOKING AT THE SUPPLIER CHAIN

Supplier Chain

CASE STUDIES

> *"Where environmental initiatives save money, then the customer is likely to be one of those reaping the rewards"*

Environmental issues do not stop at the factory gate, or at the boundaries of an individual company. Every company is part of a chain of suppliers and customers. Having considered environmental initiatives at the company level, the next logical step is to consider the performance of suppliers. For some this might mean taking a company out of the supplier base altogether if it is clear that environmental performance can never be up to scratch. More likely, however, is an approach where a company takes pains to find out what its suppliers are doing, and then helps them to develop their own policies and initiatives. Where environmental initiatives save money, then the customer is likely to be one of those reaping the rewards.

Supplier initiatives are likely to be particularly helpful to small supplier companies. Implementing a comprehensive environmental programme is undoubtedly harder for small companies than for large companies, particularly where it involves finding staff time and capital outlay. If pressure, ideally accompanied by assistance, is coming from larger companies the outlays will be easier to justify and impetus stronger. The examples drawn together here show the extent to which some companies already see their credibility resting on not just their own activities, but on those of everyone with whom they are involved.

British Telecommunications plc sees its **Supplier Programme** as an integral part of its environmental policy. BT has a formal policy of "product stewardship", i.e. aiming to minimise the whole life environmental impacts of the main products BT purchases and either sells on or ultimately discards. BT is the biggest civilian procurer of goods and services in the UK and as Chris Tuppen, Head of Environmental Management, says, "having a supplier programme is an essential component of our stance on product stewardship". As part of the programme, BT has, since early 1991, been working on a Generic Environmental Impact Standard as a means of assessing the environmental impacts of specific products and services, and also as a way of guiding suppliers towards more environmentally aware practices. In 1993 BT received an RSA Environmental Management Award for its procurement operations.

The Generic Environmental Impact Standard (GS13) is sent to companies tendering for business. The standard asks for information on the company's environmental policy and management systems as well as information about environmental impacts of the product during its whole life-cycle. This includes packaging, the ease with which the product can be recycled, any hazards arising from disposal and whether the product's use involves any emissions which will have adverse environmental effects. The answers to these questions are scored and the responses are then taken into account alongside financial and quality criteria in making a final decision on a supplier. The main usefulness of GS13 is in comparing different suppliers who are quoting against the same tender specification.

GS13 is at present limited to tenders over £750,000 which covers some 50% of the value of supplies to BT, a figure in excess of £2 billion per year. Chris Tuppen admits that BT's group procurement services do not yet have systems to measure how many contracts the standard has been applied to, but he is confident that it is widely used, "Whenever I meet big suppliers they tend to mention GS13. It is clearly having an influence on thinking".

Since 1992 BT has also run an Environmental Supplier Award, which recognises supplier environmental achievements and encourages improvements. The 1993/94 awards went to a small/medium-sized enterprise that had switched from solvent-based inking systems to processes using ultra-violet light; and a specialist waste management company. The entries are scrutinised by independent judges drawn from a wide range of business and non-business sectors. Short-listed entries are validated by site audits. The link with education is maintained through a student competition to design the trophy awarded to the overall winners.

> *"...product stewardship, and the efforts to improve supplier environmental performance, have both business and environmental benefits"*

Chris Tuppen is clear that BT's corporate goal of product stewardship, and the efforts to improve supplier environmental performance, have both business and environmental benefits. The policy has been formed with a view to minimising future costs, especially disposal and maintenance costs and energy consumption. It should also help to ensure continuity of supply, "If you're buying equipment or materials from suppliers that are not environmentally responsible you may, in years to come, find that the supply relationship is no longer tenable. There are also the benefits of buying quality - a company that has a good environmental policy and programme is likely to be a quality company".

Paper Back Limited, a small company trading in recycled paper products and office accessories, has begun to ask its suppliers to comply with a **set of environmental criteria** which it is developing. By doing this the company believes it is not only re-affirming its environmental commitment, but keeping ahead of legislation which will require consideration of product impacts.

The company sends a questionnaire to its paper suppliers, asking about issues such as energy consumption and emissions to air and water in the manufacturing process. Paper Back makes the information it receives available to clients.

Jan Kuiper, Business Development Manager, says that some suppliers are not as flexible as Paper Back would wish them to be, and as a small company with a turnover of less than £3 million, it is not easy to encourage suppliers to change their processes or beliefs. "If you are a multi-national company and have 2,000 suppliers you can put more pressure on them. We rely on 10 or 12 at most on the printing side so it is difficult to drop them. But we make life more difficult for them and demand more."

Paper Back sees that environmental legislation which has been passed over the last 20 years, both at a national and European level, has been in favour of better recycling and reduction of waste and pollution levels. Therefore, companies are faced increasingly with pressures to adopt processes with a less-damaging environmental impact, and to look more closely at the whole life-cycle of their products from raw materials to production processes, distribution and disposal. By questioning suppliers, Paper Back is establishing a format that will not only benefit it as a company, but will also ultimately benefit the suppliers themselves.

Scott Limited, the UK's largest producer of tissue products, has developed a **comprehensive supplier environmental audit** in the belief that it will benefit the long term health of the business.

At the end of the 1980s, Scott realised that consumer concern about environmental issues was increasing, and manufacturers were marketing their products with an environmental slant. Scott set up an environmental unit to develop a response. Martin Kybert, Environmental Affairs Manager, says that as different issues such as recycling, chlorine bleaching and forestry practices surfaced, "it made me think of playing football in the school playground - someone would kick the ball to one end and everybody would go chasing after it, then someone would kick it to the other end and we'd all run after it again. That was not a sensible way to go about following these issues, always running behind, so we decided to take a more holistic approach".

It was clear that, in the life-cycle of a product, there were many environmental impacts that were outside Scott's direct control. However, the fact that the company has an indirect involvement in all stages of production, when seen from the market place, encouraged Scott to take responsibility for its products further up the chain. The company decided it could not deal with its suppliers as it had done before, purely on the basis of cost, quality and service issues, and that an environmental dimension had to be added.

As a manufacturer of paper products, Scott had two advantages when formulating a supplier audit. Firstly, the company uses one major raw material which is pulp, so the difficulties of comparing unlike products, and of developing a suitable format for the audit, were reduced. Secondly, Scott is the largest tissue manufacturer in Europe which translates into strong purchasing power.

The result is three questionnaires that comprehensively examine a supplier's environmental impacts. The first two, one for potential suppliers and one for existing suppliers, ask about emissions, use of energy, water and chemicals, wood source, solid waste and forestry management. The third covers supplier forestry operations and gives Scott useful background information on suppliers' forestry management processes. However, Martin Kybert says, "When it comes to forestry, there is no substitute for looking at it on the ground. From this year we will be doing an on the spot assessment of all our suppliers - it's a truly ground-breaking piece of work". Based on work begun by the Forestry Stewardship Council, Scott will use experts to audit forests on the basis of regulation and compliance, social and economic aspects and environmental impacts of forestry operations.

"We are keeping ahead and we believe we will get our reward from extra sales".

The format of the audit and the questionnaires gives Scott a measure for each supplier which can be plotted on a scale of performance. Using this information Scott is able to determine those suppliers with whom it wishes to do business. The company has decided it will not deal with those in the bottom 10%. Martin Kybert says, "What we are looking for is lowest cost, perfect quality, great service and best on the environment, but in reality there is a trading off that goes on across all of those dimensions".

The company is undertaking this work for the benefit of its business, based on its analysis of consumers' perceptions about environmental impacts and possible future legislation involving "cradle to grave" scrutiny of all aspects of a product. Martin Kybert comments, "We believe that what we are doing is the right thing to do - it is good for our business in the long term. We are keeping ahead and we believe we will get our reward from extra sales."

Skippingdale Paper Products Ltd, who make nappies for major UK and Scandinavian retailers to package as their own brands, has a policy of only purchasing wood pulp from well managed forests. The majority of its pulp comes from Sweden where sensitive forest management is a legal requirement - for example, for every tree cut down three more must be planted. The majority of tissue fibre also comes from Sweden, and is only purchased from suppliers whose manufacturing processes meet the strict guidelines of the Swedish Environmental Association, which covers air and effluent emissions.

The pulp industry has also been criticised for using chlorine gas in bleaching which results in the production of chloro-organic compounds, some of which, even in small quantities, are considered toxic. Paper product manufacturers are increasingly using pulp bleached with chlorine dioxide instead of chlorine gas, a method which minimises the production of chlorinated by-products. These are called Elemental Chlorine Free (ECF) pulps. Skippingale switched completely to using ECF pulps in 1989, to satisfy the requirements of the more stringent Scandinavian market. Dialogue and information-sharing with suppliers have always been important to

Skippingdale, and together with visits to check on forest management, have proved to be sufficient in keeping abreast of supplier environmental performance. This has been met with positive reactions from suppliers. Skippingdale's suppliers have benefited by maintaining its custom and, likewise, Skippingdale has benefited by maintaining the custom of the retailers it supplies who increasingly scrutinise their suppliers' environmental performance. Managing Director, Mats Akesson, says, "We see this as being vital in maintaining our business viability".

Monitoring current and prospective suppliers' compliance with environmental legislation is crucial to **Nissan Motor Manufacturing (UK) Ltd** (NMUK). "The worst scenario for us would be for a supplier's activities to be suspended by the appropriate regulatory authority due to non-compliance. This can have a significant impact on our own production, so it is important for us to establish where the risks are", says Bob Gray, Purchasing Manager. In 1993 NMUK carried out a survey of UK based suppliers' compliance with the Environmental Protection Act. The survey also monitored changes in supplier processes that may have a knock-on effect on NMUK's own in-house processes. "Otherwise we could, for example, start releasing unexpected emissions due to the fact that a supplier has changed the ingredients of one of our materials", says Bob Gray. The company surveyed those suppliers most likely to experience difficulties in complying or whose processes they wanted to understand more thoroughly.

Following on from this NMUK has now incorporated an environmental monitor with the traditional cost, quality and delivery considerations when assessing prospective suppliers or when reviewing existing suppliers, as new models or model changes are introduced. All suppliers are asked if their activities comply with the environmental legislation of the country in which they are operating, and with Europe-wide legislation if applicable.

There are several examples of NMUK's environmental initiatives which have gone beyond legal requirements and which could not have been taken forward without the commitment of suppliers. One is returnable packaging. The company now receives 96% of components in re-usable containers (see page 46). Bob Gray says, "Initially we met with some resistance from suppliers. However, by working closely with them to demonstrate the benefits that can be realised we have come as far as we have". Suppliers benefit, for instance, by improving operational efficiency through no longer having to assemble cardboard boxes. "The savings made in some cases have cancelled out a supplier's increased costs which would otherwise have formed an increase in component price to NMUK. So the savings can be passed on to us without eroding the company's profit margin."

According to Bob Gray, "We see our suppliers as partners and place a strong emphasis on working together to improve overall capability. Environmental issues are an integral part of this performance and should a supplier's ability to meet environmental legislation threaten its processes or ability to supply we would look to assist, in partnership, to resolve the situation. This partnership approach has worked well. In fact we have reaped the benefits as suppliers are much more proactive, suggesting alternative or improved methods. For instance, they have approached us with improved returnable packaging".

In the long term NMUK is hoping to collaborate with others in its industry to further improve supplier performance. This will help prevent suppliers getting different messages from different customers. "A start has been made with an industry forum called ACORD (Automotive Consortium on Recycling and Disposal - see page 37) aimed at recycling as much as possible from old vehicles", says Dr Les Nicholls, Chairman of the Environment Planning Group.

"We see our suppliers as partners and place a strong emphasis on working together..."

Triplex Safety Glass Ltd., the automotive glass manufacturers (part of the Pilkington Group) was giving its customers an environmental and a cost problem by packing glass with a sheet of paper between each layer. The paper was also a cost to Triplex - the paper for a year's supply of door glass for one particular car model costs £110,000. At the other end, the customer would have to pay for its disposal. The answer was to develop re-usable pallets to transport the glass - the glass is now lifted out and the pallets returned for the next run. This development meant a capital outlay, but it has paid for itself in paper in one year. More than this, as far as Derek Norman, Pilkington's Director of Environmental Affairs, is concerned, if the customer wants a product with minimal packaging, the outlay amounts to the cost of keeping that customer's business. Derek Norman thinks that this approach to packaging and transportation will become standard.

"We have to change our attitude to purchasing"

As a customer itself, **Forte Plc** sees the need to change its own thinking. John Forte, Environmental Services Director, says, "We must start talking about waste as a valuable resource, a commodity, not a valueless thing. It comes back to the customer. We have to change our attitude to purchasing and be prepared to buy things in future that contain an element of recycled product or, best of all, are made totally from recycled products. So, for example, there is nothing to stop us considering very seriously buying fencing made of recycled polystyrene for our sites".

Forte's experience has been that, faced with a request for change in a product, suppliers tend to put obstacles in the way - usually saying that it will mean a higher price. John Forte comments, "In a lot of cases to change attitudes, one company is not sufficient - you need the muscle of several companies. Individual companies will always be faced with the problem that if one is asking for something different, they will have to pay a premium for it. Eventually others catch up and benefit from our lead".

BP Chemicals Limited had considerable difficulty in persuading valve suppliers to fit a packing material that significantly reduced the emissions of VOCs from its high pressure hydrocarbon pipelines. BP Chemicals' public commitment to reduce air emissions by 50% between 1990 and 1997 means that cleaner technology is a vital concern.

After a comprehensive testing programme of available alternatives to the traditionally used asbestos material (see page 33), BP Chemicals went to the suppliers of valves with results that demonstrated a clear environmental benefit. Suppliers were used to fitting valves with packing based on economic considerations alone, in other words, the cheapest material. Although BP was a large customer, and was prepared to pay more to receive a superior product, the company had to apply considerable pressure to persuade suppliers to change over. Hedley Jenkins, Technology Manager, says, "It [valve supply] is a very competitive industry. It is like having to have legislation to fit seat-belts in cars - everybody agrees it is a good idea, but it makes the car more expensive, hence the necessity for outside customer pressure".

BP Chemicals has now taken the decision not to buy valves unless they are fitted with one of the two best packing materials tested by the company. It now looks at the combination of the best valves with the best packing, in order to achieve the greatest possible overall environmental and economic benefits. The company is also reducing the number of valve suppliers and will therefore get better commercial deals from larger orders, further enhancing the economic advantages.

"As the DIY market leader, **B&Q plc** has a responsibility to lead and an opportunity to profit by being ahead of its competitors on a course that they will inevitably be required to follow."

This is the approach that led B&Q to launch an environmental programme in 1991, which includes a comprehensive **Supplier Environmental Audit**. In order to understand the environmental impacts of a particular product, it is important to consider the entire life-cycle from the extraction of the raw materials to the disposal methods. B&Q believes that by auditing suppliers and choosing to sell one product rather than another, or by purchasing from one manufacturer rather than another, the company can have a significant effect on the environmental impact of the products it sells.

> *"...by auditing suppliers and choosing to sell one product rather than another, or by purchasing from one manufacturer rather than another, the company can have a significant effect on the environmental impact of the products it sells"*

The environmental impacts of manufacturing include energy use, resource consumption, emissions to land, water and air and waste generation. B&Q's intention is "ultimately to buy only from suppliers who understand the major impacts of their products and show a real commitment to reducing them in a realistic time scale".

B&Q's policy now requires all suppliers to produce a written statement outlining their environmental impacts and actions to reduce them. For example, suppliers are required to specify post-consumer, recycled materials for packaging wherever possible. All suppliers have to complete a detailed 40-page questionnaire which covers a wide range of issues such as environmental management practices, energy efficiency, waste policies, packaging and raw material sources. Companies are then rated by company environmental commitment. B&Q also encourages its suppliers, in turn, to audit their own suppliers, so environmental impacts are assessed as far up the supplier chain as possible. Suppliers will undergo a six-monthly review, due to the rapid pace of change in the environmental debate.

The company's environmental policy states, "B&Q will de-list suppliers who show no commitment to improving their environmental performance". In practice, suppliers recognise the value of B&Q as a large buyer, and where problems have arisen with a supplier's environmental performance, B&Q's buyers are usually able to address a problem with the supplier concerned to bring the company up to the required standard. De-listing tends to occur where a combination of poor quality, service and environmental performance coincide. However, B&Q have dropped a number of its products as a result of its auditing process, such as Brazilian mahogany, certain fire extinguishers, and peat extracted from Sites of Special Scientific Interest (see page 88). In 1993 B&Q won an RSA Environmental Management Award for its Supplier Environmental Audit.

> *"...the emphasis in the environmental debate concerning developing countries will move towards this approach..."*

B&Q is now working on extending its audit to examine the social impacts of its products, such as working conditions in factories, health and political rights. Alan Knight, Environmental Policy Controller, believes that the emphasis in the environmental debate concerning developing countries will move towards this approach, "If you look after the people, the environment will look after itself". By integrating such a comprehensive examination of all its products into its normal buying process, B&Q believes that it can stay ahead of the competition and anticipate legislation, allowing it more control over its business management.

According to Alan Smith, Managing Director, "It is not always possible to look for immediate payback on environmental progress, but I firmly believe that it is in our interests as a business to be an environmental leader in the retail sector".

APPENDIX 1

Company Summary Information

Name of company:	**Acme United Limited**
Nature of business:	Manufacture of scissors and knives
Scale of operations in UK:	One site
Turnover in 1993:	£3.2 million
Number of employees in UK:	70
Name of parent company or group:	Acme United Corporation, USA
Savings / initiatives featured:	New business opportunity: recycled kitchen utensils and cosmetic products (see page 57)

Name of company:	**Alfer Limited**
Nature of business:	Foundry
Scale of operations in UK:	One site
Turnover in 1993:	£71.5 million (Baxi Partnership Limited)
Number of employees in UK:	120
Name of parent company or group:	Baxi Partnership Limited
Savings / initiatives featured:	Recycling: savings of up to £50,000 per year (see page 38)

Name of company:	**Ambler of Ballyclare**
Nature of business:	Worsted spinning
Scale of operations in UK:	One site
Turnover in 1993:	Not available
Number of employees in UK:	280
Name of parent company or group:	Coats Viyella Plc
Savings / initiatives featured:	Packaging reduction: savings of £18,000 per year (see page 47)

Name of company:	**Anaplast Ltd**
Nature of business:	Manufacture of polythene packaging
Scale of operations in UK:	Two sites
Turnover in 1993:	£192.5 million (British Polythene Industries Plc)
Number of employees in UK:	280
Name of parent company or group:	British Polythene Industries Plc
Savings / initiatives featured:	Recycling polythene packaging (see page 42)

Name of company:	**Arjo Wiggins Fine Papers Limited**
Nature of business:	Paper manufacture
Scale of operations in UK:	Three sites
Turnover in 1993:	£210 million
Number of employees:	1,725 (includes France)
Name of parent company or group:	Arjo Wiggins Appleton Plc
Savings / initiatives featured:	Savings over a three-year period of £270,000 by using less water and reducing effluent losses (see page 28)

Name of company:	**B & Q plc**
Nature of business:	DIY retailer
Scale of operations in UK:	280 sites
Turnover in 1993:	£1,000 million
Number of employees in UK:	15,000
Name of parent company or group:	Kingfisher Plc
Savings / initiatives featured:	Supplier environmental audit (see page 60) Markets for more environmentally sensitive products (see page 68)

Name of company:	**Bayer plc**
Nature of business:	Manufacture of chemicals and pharmaceuticals
Scale of operations in UK:	Seven sites
Turnover in 1993:	£700 million
Number of employees in UK:	2,700
Name of parent company or group:	Bayer AG, Germany
Savings / initiatives featured:	Water use: saving 15-20% at one site (see page 25)

Name of company:	**Blue Circle Industries Plc**
Nature of business:	Manufacture and sale of heavy building materials and home products (e.g. cookers and central heating equipment)
Scale of operations in UK:	Approximately 60
Turnover in 1993:	£1,678.8 million
Number of employees in UK:	9,468
Savings / initiatives featured:	Energy: saving 3-5% of annual costs on cement kilns fitted with computerised control systems (see page 19)

Name of company:	**Blue Circle Waste Management Limited**
Nature of business:	Waste management through landfill and incineration operations, and manufacture of energy and effluent treatment equipment
Scale of operations in UK:	16 sites (11 of which are landfill)
Turnover in 1993:	£34 million
Number of employees in UK:	220
Name of parent company or group:	Blue Circle Industries Plc
Savings / initiatives featured:	Energy: burning landfill gas to produce electricity (see page 18)

Name of company:	**Bluecrest Convenience Foods Limited**
Nature of business:	Manufacture of ready meals
Scale of operations in UK:	One site
Turnover in 1993:	£20 million
Number of employees in UK:	300
Name of parent company or group:	Booker Plc
Savings / initiatives featured:	Improved effluent management: savings of £60,000 a year (see page 27) Also initiatives on energy (see pages 20 & 21) and packaging (see page 46)

Name of company:	**BMW (GB) Limited**
Nature of business:	Car manufacture
Scale of operations in UK:	160 sites
Turnover in 1993:	DM 29,016 million (BMW AG)
Number of employees in UK:	350
Name of parent company or group:	BMW AG
Savings / initiatives featured:	Establishment of a car recycling plant (see page 40)

Name of company:	**BOC Gases Europe**
Nature of business:	Industrial gases
Scale of operations in UK:	100 sites
Turnover in 1993:	£3.2 billion (The BOC Group plc)
Number of employees in UK:	12,500
Name of parent company or group:	The BOC Group plc
Savings / initiatives featured:	UK market leader in cleaner soldering technology (see page 55)

Name of company:	**Boots The Chemists Ltd**
Nature of business:	Retail chemists
Scale of operations in UK:	1,200 stores
Turnover in 1993/4:	£2,808 million
Number of employees in UK:	Over 50,000
Name of parent company or group:	The Boots Company Plc
Savings / initiatives featured:	Packaging audit (see page 48) and increased market share (see page 60)

Name of company:	**BP Chemicals Limited**
Nature of business:	Manufacture and marketing of chemicals and plastics
Scale of operations in UK:	Four major sites and a number of smaller sites
Turnover in 1993:	£2,934 million
Number of employees in UK:	6,050
Name of parent company or group:	British Petroleum Plc
Savings / initiatives featured:	Waste reduction: savings of £100,000 per annum (see page 32) Soil contamination identification (see page 36) Work with suppliers (see page 67)

Name of company:	**British Telecommunications plc (BT)**
Nature of business:	Telecommunication products and services
Scale of operations in UK:	Approximately 8,000 sites
Turnover in 1993/4:	£13.7 billion
Number of employees in UK:	156,000
Savings / initiatives featured:	Supplier initiative (see page 63)

Name of company:	**Coats Viyella Plc**
Nature of business:	Manufacture, processing and distribution of industrial and domestic sewing thread, homewares, fashion wares, knitwear, garments, yarns and fabrics and precision engineering
Scale of operations in UK:	Over 100 manufacturing sites
Turnover in 1993:	£2,444 million
Number of employees in UK:	27,654
Savings / initiatives featured:	Energy: two initiatives yielding savings of £25,000 and £12,000 per year (see pages 21 & 20) Packaging reduction: savings of £100,000 per year (see page 47)

Name of company:	**The Co-operative Bank plc**
Nature of business:	Banking
Scale of operations in UK:	109 branches and 3,000 banking points at Co-operative retail societies
Assets in 1993:	£3.4 billion
Number of employees in UK:	3,886
Name of parent company or group:	CWS Limited
Savings / initiatives featured:	Improved performance since launching ethical policy (see page 60)

Name of company:	**DHL International (UK) Limited**
Nature of business:	International express carriage
Scale of operations in UK:	38 sites
Turnover in 1993:	Not available
Number of employees in UK:	2,000
Savings / initiatives featured:	Cutting down on unnecessary transport: projected saving of £358,000 over three years (see page 50)

Name of company:	**Edwards High Vacuum International**
Nature of business:	Design, manufacture and marketing of vacuum equipment
Scale of operations in UK:	Four manufacturing sites
Turnover in 1993:	£3.2 billion (The BOC Group plc)
Number of employees in UK:	1,100
Name of parent company or group:	The BOC Group plc
Savings / initiatives featured:	New business opportunity: dry vacuum pumps which eliminate contaminated effluent at source (see page 55)

Name of company:	**Elm Energy & Recycling (UK) Limited**
Nature of business:	Electricity generation from scrap tyres
Scale of operations in UK:	One site
Turnover in 1993:	Not available as scheme started operating in October 1993
Number of employees in UK:	95
Name of parent company or group:	Nipsco Industries Inc, USA
Savings / initiatives featured:	New business opportunity: energy from scrap tyres (see page 54)

Name of company:	**Esso UK plc**
Nature of business:	With two operating companies, Esso Exploration and Production UK Limited, responsible for the exploration and production of crude oil and natural gas, and Esso Petroleum Company Ltd, responsible for refining and distribution of petroleum products throughout the UK
Scale of operations in UK:	Six main sites and a number of bulk plants and distribution terminals
Turnover in 1993:	£6,608 million (gross)
Number of employees in UK:	4,158
Name of parent company or group:	Exxon Corporation
Savings / initiatives featured:	Energy: estimated saving at one site of £1,500 in 1993 (see page 23) Recovering over 4 million litres of petroleum annually through reducing vapour emissions (see page 33)

Name of company:	**Forte Plc**
Nature of business:	Hotels and restaurants
Scale of operations in UK:	Approximately 1,000 operations
Turnover in 1993:	£2 billion
Number of employees in UK:	40,000
Savings / initiatives featured:	Energy: savings of £180,000 in 1993 (see page 15) Also waste reduction (see page 32) and supplier initiatives (see page 67)

Name of company:	**Glaxo Holdings p.l.c.** (of which Glaxochem Ltd is a wholly-owned subsidiary)
Nature of business:	Pharmaceuticals
Scale of operations in the UK:	10 sites
Turnover in 1993:	£1,968 million (Europe)
Number of employees in the UK:	12,149
Savings / initiatives featured:	Waste reduction: savings of £1 million per year (see page 35)

Name of company:	**Greenpeace International Ltd**
Nature of business:	Independent environmental pressure group
Scale of operations in UK:	One central office
Turnover in 1993:	Income derived solely from supporters and the public
Number of employees in UK:	90
Savings / initiatives featured:	New business opportunity: CFC/HFC/HCFC-free fridges (see page 56)

Name of company:	**Lambson Fine Chemicals Ltd**
Nature of business:	Organic chemical manufacture, sulphuric acid and acid sales
Scale of operations in UK:	Two sites
Turnover in 1993:	£25 million
Number of employees in UK:	300
Name of parent company or group:	Lambson Group Limited
Savings / initiatives featured:	Waste reduction: savings of £90,000 per year (see page 34)

Name of company:	**Lloyds Bank Plc**
Nature of business:	Financial services
Scale of operations in UK:	2,400 locations
Total income in 1993:	£3,974 million
Number of employees in UK:	44,000
Name of parent company or group:	Lloyds Bank Group
Savings / initiatives featured:	Sale of electricity to the value of £10,000 in four months by operating a CHP plant (see page 20)

Name of Company:	**Matsushita Electric (UK) Ltd**
Nature of business:	Manufacture of electronic products
Scale of operations in UK:	One site
Turnover in 1993:	£220 million
Number of employees in UK:	1,600
Name of parent company or group:	Matsushita Electric Industrial Co. Ltd., Osaka, Japan
Savings / initiatives featured:	Recycling: expect to save £100,000 per year by 1995 (see page 41)

Name of company:	**National Westminster Bank Plc**
Nature of business:	International financial institution
Scale of operations in UK:	3,500 premises
Operating income in 1993:	£6,995 million
Number of employees in UK:	Approximately 70,000
Savings / initiatives featured:	Energy: savings of £630,000 per year (see page 22) Waste reduction: computer printout review (see page 31) Compacting waste paper with estimated financial advantage of £640,000 over five years (see page 52)

Name of company:	**Nissan Motor Manufacturing (UK) Limited**
Nature of business:	Manufacture of motor vehicles and automotive components
Scale of operations in UK:	One manufacturing site
Turnover in 1993:	£1.3 billion
Number of employees in UK:	4,250 (end December 1993)
Name of parent company or group:	Nissan Motor Company Ltd
Savings / initiatives featured:	Recycling: savings in excess of £700,000 in 1993 (see page 38) Also packaging (see page 46) and supplier initiatives (see page 66)

Name of company:	**Paper Back Limited**
Nature of business:	Recycled paper merchants
Scale of operations in UK:	Head office in London, sales offices in Sheffield and Birmingham
Turnover in 1993:	£2.8 million
Number of employees in UK:	26
Savings / initiatives featured:	New business opportunity: recycled paper (see page 58) Supplier initiatives (see page 64)

Name of company:	**Procter & Gamble Limited**
Nature of business:	Manufacture and marketing of detergent and personal care items
Scale of operations in UK:	Three factories, four administration sites and two research and development facilities
Turnover in 1992/3:	£1,377 million
Number of employees in UK:	5,000
Name of parent company or group:	The Procter & Gamble Company
Savings / initiatives featured:	Cutting down on unnecessary transport: reduced number of lorry journeys by 16,500 (see page 52) Packaging reduction: cost benefits to customer (see page 49)

Name of company:	**Ricoh UK Products Ltd**
Nature of business:	Manufacture of office automation equipment and supplies
Scale of operations in UK:	One site
Turnover in 1993:	£50 million
Number of employees in UK:	550
Name of parent company or group:	Ricoh Company, Japan
Savings / initiatives featured:	Recycling: reduced manufacturing costs on one product line by 54% (see page 43)

Name of company:	**Scott Limited**
Nature of business:	Manufacture and sale of disposable tissue products
Scale of operations in UK:	Two paper mills, plus head office and distribution depots
Turnover in 1993:	Over £300 million
Number of employees in UK:	1,800
Name of parent company or group:	Scott Paper Company of Philadelphia
Savings / initiatives featured:	Using less water: 40% reduction at one mill (see page 29) Supplier auditing initiative (see page 64)

Name of company:	**Simpson Wright and Lowe (sock division)**
Nature of business:	Sock manufacture
Scale of operations in UK:	One site
Turnover in 1993:	£19 million
Number of employees in UK:	480
Name of parent company or group:	Coats Viyella Plc
Savings / initiatives featured:	Waste reduction: savings of £100,000 on materials and production costs (see page 32)

Name of company:	**Skippingdale Paper Products Ltd**
Nature of business:	Manufacture of disposable nappies
Scale of operations in UK:	Two sites
Turnover in 1993:	£19 million
Number of employees in UK:	180
Savings / initiatives featured:	Cutting down on unnecessary transport: savings of £195,000 per year (see page 51)
	Waste reduction: savings of £800,000 per year (see page 35)
	Also work with suppliers (see page 65)

Name of company:	**Southern Water Services Ltd**
Nature of business:	Provision of water and waste water services in Kent, Sussex, Hampshire and the Isle of Wight
Scale of operations in UK:	1,020 sites
Turnover in 1993:	£350 million
Number of employees in UK:	3,500
Name of parent company or group:	Southern Water Plc
Savings / initiatives featured:	Energy: saving £36,000 per year (see page 16)

Name of company:	**Spring Grove Services Ltd**
Nature of business:	Industrial/commercial laundry
Scale of operations in UK:	14 sites
Turnover in 1993:	£90 million
Number of employees in UK:	2,200
Name of parent company or group:	Granada Plc
Savings / initiatives featured:	Energy: anticipates savings of £12,000 per year (see page 21)
	Using less water and energy: savings of £30,000 per year (see page 26)
	Anticipates elimination of effluent charges (see page 28)

Name of company:	**Standard Products Ltd UK**
Nature of business:	Manufacture of automotive rubber and plastic parts
Scale of operations in UK:	4 divisions
Turnover in 1993:	£49 million
Number of employees in UK:	1,200
Savings / initiatives featured:	Recycling: disposal costs reduced from £30,000 per month to £5,000 (see page 39)

Name of company:	**The Standish Co**
Nature of business:	Dyeing and finishing of textiles
Scale of operations in UK:	One site
Turnover in 1993:	£9.7 million
Number of employees in UK:	197
Name of parent company or group:	Coats Viyella Plc
Savings / initiatives featured:	Recycling heated water: savings of £100,000 per year on energy and water processing costs (see page 25)

Name of company:	**TNT Express (U.K.) Limited**
Nature of business:	Transport distribution and logistics
Scale of operations in UK:	Over 400 locations
Turnover in 1993:	Over £270 million
Number of employees in UK:	6,500
Name of parent company or group:	TNT Limited (Australia)
Savings / initiatives featured:	Saving 17% of annual fuel used through improved vehicle design and aerodynamics (see page 52)

Name of company:	**Triplex Safety Glass Ltd.**
Nature of business:	Automotive glazing
Scale of operations in UK:	Two sites
Turnover in 1993:	£75 million
Number of employees in UK:	1,400
Name of parent company or group:	Pilkington Plc
Savings / initiatives featured:	Energy: anticipates savings of up to £200,000 in 1994 (see page 19) Recycling: annual financial benefit of £273,890 (see page 39) Also waste reduction (see page 31) and work with customers (see page 67)

Name of company:	**Varta Ltd**
Nature of business:	Battery manufacture
Scale of operations in UK:	One consumer sales office and one battery assembly plant
Turnover in 1993:	£15 million
Number of employees in UK:	109
Name of parent company or group:	Varta Batterie A.G.
Savings / initiatives featured:	Attributes market position to the innovative way it has approached the market and to a succession of environmental initiatives (see page 62)

Name of company:	**Wade Furniture Ltd**
Nature of business:	Reproduction cabinet furniture in mahogany, yew and lined oak
Scale of operations in UK:	One site
Number of employees in UK:	100
Name of parent company or group:	Wade Furniture Group Ltd
Savings / initiatives featured:	New product initiative avoiding the use of tropical timbers (see page 59)

APPENDIX 2

Further Information

Advisory Committee on Business and the Environment (ACBE)
DTI, Ashdown House, 123 Victoria Street, London SW1E 6RB;
Tel: DTI 071 215 1042 or DOE 071 276 3732

An advisory committee established jointly by the Department of the Environment and the
Department of Trade and Industry in May 1991 to provide a strategic level dialogue between
Government and business on environmental issues. (See Appendix Three - Publications)

Association for the Conservation of Energy (ACE)
9 Sherlock Mews, London W1M 3RH; Tel: 071 935 1495

ACE was established in 1981 by a number of major companies active within the energy conservation
industry. ACE encourages a positive national awareness of the need for and benefits of energy
conservation and works for a consistent national policy and increased investment in all appropriate
energy saving measures.

Automotive Consortium on Recycling and Disposal (ACORD)
Forbes House, Halkin Street, London SW1X 7DS; Tel: 071 235 7000

ACORD was set up under the umbrella of the Society of Motor Manufacturers and Traders Ltd
(SMMT) to establish and implement a multi-industry strategy to achieve improvements in the scrap
vehicle disposal process. (See Car Recycling, page 37)

British Plastics Federation (BPF)
6 Bath Place, Rivington Street, London EC2A 3JE; Tel: 071 457 5000

The BPF is the trade association for the UK plastics industry. BPF has carried out work on recycling
and energy generation from waste.

British Standards Institution
Linford House, Milton Keynes, MK14 6LE; Tel: 0908 221166

The BSI Standards Catalogue shows many standards relating to environmental protection. It has
published the world's first standard for environmental management systems (BS 7750) which has
clear parallels with the BS 5750 on quality management.

Building Research Energy Conservation Support Unit (BRESCU)
Building Research Establishment, Bucknalls Lane, Garston, Watford, Herts WD2 7JR;
Tel: 0923 66425

The Building Research Establishment (BRE) is an Executive Agency of the Department of the
Environment (See BREEAM - page 87). BRESCU provides information and advice on energy
conservation in buildings.

Business in the Environment (BiE)
8 Stratton Street, London W1X 5FD; Tel: 071 629 1600

Business in the Environment aims to extend business leaders' awareness of environmental issues and
to provide practical assistance in improving the environmental performance of business.
(See Appendix Three - Publications)

Centre for Environment and Business in Scotland (CEBIS)
58/59 Timber Bush, Edinburgh EH6 6QH; Tel: 031 555 5210

CEBIS was established in 1991 to provide impartial environmental information to businesses in Scotland.

Centre for Exploitation of Science and Technology (CEST)
5 Berners Road, London N1 0PW; Tel: 071 354 9942

CEST is an independent non-profit making organisation working with industry, academics and government policy makers. CEST projects are designed to help companies identify new opportunities early and reduce payback periods. (See Aire & Calder Project, page 24)

Chartered Institute of Purchasing and Supply (CIPS)
Easton House, Church Street, Easton-on-the-Hill, Stamford, Lincolnshire PE9 3NZ; Tel: 0780 56777

CIPS holds conferences on environmental issues relating to purchasing and supply and have collaborated with BiE to produce the publication "Voluntary Code of Practice covering environmental performance in supplier/customer relationships".

Chemical Industries Association
King's Buildings, Smith Square, London SW1P 3JJ; Tel: 071 834 3399

The CIA's "Responsible Care" is a UK programme to help improve the chemical industry's performance in the areas of health, safety and environmental protection and to enable companies to demonstrate their improvement to the public.

Combined Heat and Power Association (CHPA)
Grosvenor Gardens House, 35/37 Grosvenor Gardens, London SW1W 0BS; Tel: 071 828 4077

The CHPA works to secure the wider use of Combined Heat and Power (CHP). It organises events and publishes and promotes technical and other information about CHP.

Confederation of British Industry Environment Business Forum
Centre Point, 103 New Oxford Street, London WC1A 1DU; Tel: 071 379 7400

The forum encourages UK companies to adopt a proactive approach to environmental issues based on the benefits to business. (See Appendix Three - Publications)

Energy Saving Trust
11-12 Buckingham Gate, London SW1E 6LB; Tel: 071 931 8401

The Energy Saving Trust is a non-profit making organisation set up by the Goverment and equally owned by the Government and utilities. It identifies, promotes and directs energy efficiency schemes in the UK.

Environment Council
21 Elizabeth Street, London SW1W 9RP Tel: 071 824 8411

A forum for individuals and organisations working towards solutions to environmental problems. The Council addresses a variety of environment issues through its meetings, events, seminars and publications. Its Business and Environment Programme is supported by over 800 companies.

The Freight Transport Association (FTA)
Hermes House, St John's Road, Tunbridge Wells, Kent TN4 9UZ; Tel: 0892 526171

The FTA has been involved in work on fuel management with the Energy Efficiency Office at the Department of the Environment.

Groundwork Foundation
85-87 Cornwall Street, Birmingham B3 3BY; Tel: 021 236 8565

The Foundation and its Trusts are working towards environmental regeneration, by linking industry with local groups. The Groundwork environmental review service is a resource for companies wanting to make a start on assessing their environmental performance.

Industry Council for Packaging and the Environment
3 Tenterden Street, London W1R 9AH; Tel: 071 409 0949

The Council was formed to bring together all sectors of industry involved in the manufacture of packaging and manufacture and retailing of packaged goods. It provides information on legislation and new technology relating to packaging and recycling of all packaging materials.

Institute of Directors (IOD)
116 Pall Mall, London SW1Y 5ED; Tel: 071 839 1233

The IOD comprises individual directors from companies of all sizes and represents the interests of its members to government and opinion formers. The IOD Environmental Advisory Group keeps a watching brief on environmental issues.

Institute of Environmental Assessment
Fen Road, East Kirkby, Lincolnshire PE23 4DB; Tel: 0790 763613

The Institute promotes best practice standards for environmental assessment and auditing and administers the Environmental Auditors Registration Association (EARA) scheme.

Institute of Environmental Managers
58|59 Timber Bush, Edinburgh EH6 6QH; Tel: 031 555 5334

The Institute was formed to provide a forum for the exchange of information between environmental managers. It produces a regular journal and organises seminars and workshops.

International Chamber of Commerce
14-15 Belgrave Square, London SW1X 8PS; Tel: 071 823 2811

ICC UNITED KINGDOM is the British affiliate of the world organisation concerned with international business issues and practice. Through its Business Charter for Sustainable Development ICC seeks to spread good environmental practice throughout business. ICC established the World Industry Council for the Environment after the Earth Summit to address environmental issues of international relevance. (See Appendix Three - Publications)

National Rivers Authority

The NRA is the Government agency controlling the pollution of rivers, estuaries and bathing waters. The NRA also manages water resources.

NRA Offices:

Northumbria	*091 213 0266*
Severn Trent	*021 711 2324*
South West	*0392 444000*
Welsh	*0222 770088*
Yorkshire	*0532 440191*
Anglian	*0733 371811*
North West	*0925 53999*
Southern	*0903 820692*
Thames	*0734 535000*
Wessex	*0278 457333*

Producer Responsibility Industry Group (packaging)

PRG Information Office, 5th Floor, Villiers House, 41-47 The Strand, London WC2 5QB; Tel: 071 839 1144

The Group was formed in 1993 from a group of Britain's leading companies in response to a challenge from the Secretary of State for the Environment issued in September 1993. The challenge was to submit a plan to "recover (value from) between 50% and 75% of all packaging waste by the year 2000".

Queen's Award for Environmental Achievement

Bridge Place, 88/89 Eccleston Square, London SW1V 1PT Tel: 071 222 2277

The award recognises companies that have achieved a significant advance, leading to increased efficiency, in the application of technology to a production or development process in British industry or the production for sale of goods which incorporate new and advanced technological qualities.

Royal Society for the encouragement of Arts, Manufactures and Commerce (RSA) Environmental Awards

8 John Adam Street, London WC2N 6EZ; Tel: 071 930 5115

The Award is given for significant initiatives by British management in pursuit of sustainability, which seeks to eliminate the negative impacts of business on the environment while maintaining the long term viability of the business.

Shell Technology Enterprise Programme (STEP)

11 St Bride Street, London EC4A 4AS

The Programme is designed to help small and medium sized businesses take advantage of the skills and abilities of the local undergraduate population at a low cost.

United Kingdom Ecolabelling Board (UKEB)

7th Floor, Eastbury House, 30-34 Albert Embankment, London SE1 7TL; Tel: 071 820 1199

UKEB is a government body established to administer the EC scheme of environmental labelling in the UK.

Waste Management Information Bureau (WMIB)

National Environmental Technology Centre, F6 Culham, Abingdon, Oxfordshire OX14 3DB Tel: 0235 433442

WMIB provides a library and information retrieval service on non-radioactive waste management. It publishes "Waste and Environment Today" and produces the Wasteinfo database.

World Industry Council for the Environment (WICE)
40 rue Albert Ier, 75008, Paris, France

WICE is a CEO membership organisation set up by the ICC in 1993 to address key environmental issues following the Earth Summit in Rio.

UK GOVERNMENT DEPARTMENTS

DEPARTMENT OF THE ENVIRONMENT (DOE)

Enquiries	*071 276 3000*
Co-ordination of environmental policies	*071 276 8393*
Environmental Impact Assessment and planning	*071 276 3865*
Contaminated land and liabilities	*071 276 8461*
EU ECO-Management and Audit Scheme	*071 276 3377*
Business and the environment and ACBE	*071 276 3732*
Environmental Protection Technology	*071 276 3753*

Energy Efficiency Office (EEO)
Deparment of the Environment, 2 Marsham Street, London SW1P 3EB Tel: 071 276 6200

The EEO is responsible for promoting energy efficiency in industry, commerce and the public sectors. It also provides assistance towards consultancy advice for firms employing less than 500 employees under the Energy Management Assistance Scheme (see below).

Energy Management Assistance Scheme (EMAS)
Deparment of the Environment, 2 Marsham Street, London SW1P 3EB Tel: 071 276 3787

Launched in February 1992, EMAS provides help with energy management consultancy costs for small and medium sized organisations. The selection criteria for supporting applications require potential energy savings of at least 10% of energy bills.

Energy Technology Support Unit (ETSU)
Energy Efficiency Enquiries Bureau, Harwell, Oxfordshire OX11 0RA; Tel: 0235 436747
Renewable Energies Enquiries Bureau, Harwell, Oxfordshire OX11 0RA; Tel: 0235 433 601

ETSU manages the DOE's Energy Efficiency Best Practice Programme on behalf of the Energy Efficiency Office, and various programmes on renewable energies on behalf of the DTI.

Environmental Technology Best Practice Programme
Tel: DTI 071 215 1051 or DOE 071 276 3748

The scheme has the dual aim of promoting improved industrial competitiveness and reducing pollution, with a strong emphasis on reduction and elimination of waste and pollution at source. It concentrates on provision and delivery of information rather than grant assistance to firms. Priority areas will be identified by DTI/DOE in consultation with industry. To be launched in late 1994.

Her Majesty's Inspectorate of Pollution (HMIP)

Responsible for regulating the most serious polluting industrial processes under the Environment Protection Act 1990.

HMIP Offices:

Central	*071 276 8061*
East	*0234 272112*
West	*0272 319653*
North	*0532 786636*
HMIP performs a similar role in Scotland	*031 244 3062*

"Making a Corporate Commitment" Campaign
Energy Efficiency Office, Dept of the Environment, 2 Marsham Street, London SW1P 3EB;
Tel: 071 276 3568

The aim of the campaign is to encourage organisations to make a corporate commitment to energy efficiency as part of positive environmental management (see page 17).

DEPARTMENT OF TRADE AND INDUSTRY (DTI)

DTI Environment Division

The Environment Division aims to help firms to respond to environmental challenges and market opportunities.

Contacts:

Recycling	**071 215 1036**
CFCs and ozone layer	*071 215 1018*
Clean Technology	**071 215 1028**
Waste Management	*071 215 1330*
Environmental Management	**071 215 1022**

Environmental Helpline
Tel: 0800 585794

The Helpline is a DTI telephone enquiry service providing a comprehensive information service on environmental issues for business. Advice is free if the enquiry can be handled with less than four hours work.

EUREKA

EUREKA is a pan-European framework to promote commercial research and development collaboration leading to high technology products, processes or services. Eligibility for future support for project implementation will be restricted to small firms, higher education institutions and research organisations.

Joint Environmental Markets Unit (JEMU)
Tel: 071 215 1055

JEMU has been established by DTI and DOE to help raise awareness of growing environmental markets, to encourage UK companies to exploit these opportunities. Material provided includes case studies and access to market information on selected sectors.

Small Firms Merit Award for Research and Technology (SMART)

This programme offers £12 million of grants each year for feasibility studies and prototypes of innovative technological projects with commercial potential.

Support for Projects Under Research (SPUR)
Tel: 071 215 1055

SPUR was established to encourage firms to develop new products and processes which involve a significant technological advance. It is open to companies with up to 250 employees and will provide grants of up to £150,000 for 30% of eligible product costs. It is currently under review and will be restructured in 1995, the details of which are expected to be available in late 1994.

APPENDIX 3

Publications

Advisory Committee on Business and the Environment (1993)
"The Environment: A Business Guide",
DTI/DOE, London, UK

Advisory Committee on Business and the Environment (1993)
"Practical Energy Saving: a Guide for Smaller Businesses",
DTI/DOE, London, UK

Advisory Committee on Business and the Environment (1993)
"A Guide to Environmental Best Practice for Company Transport",
DTI/DOE, London, UK

Advisory Committee on Business and the Environment (1993)
"Third Progress Report",
DTI/DOE, London, UK

Bragg S, Knapp P & McLean R (1993)
"Improving Environmental Performance: A Guide to a Proven and Effective Approach",
Business and the Environment Practitioner Series, Technical Communications (Publishing) Ltd, UK

British Standards Institution (1987)
"BS 5750 - Quality Systems",
BSI Standards Board, UK

British Standards Institution (1994)
"BS 7750 - Specification for Environmental Management Systems",
BSI Standards Board, UK

Burke T & Hill J (1990)
"Ethics, Environment and the Company: A Guide to Effective Action",
The Institute of Business Ethics, London, UK

Business in the Environment (1990)
"Your Business and the Environment - An Executive Guide",
Business in the Environment, London, UK

Business in the Environment (1992)
"A Measure of Commitment - Guidelines for Measuring Environmental Performance",
Business in the Environment, London, UK

Business in the Environment (1993)
"Buying into the Environment - Guidelines for Integrating the Environment into Purchasing and Supply",
Business in the Environment, London, UK

Business in the Environment (1993)
"The LCA Sourcebook - A European Business Guide to Life-Cycle Assessment",
Business in the Environment, London, UK

CBI (1990)
"Narrowing the Gap - Environmental Auditing for Business",
CBI, London, UK

CBI (1991)
"Towards a Recycling Culture",
CBI, London, UK

CBI (1991)
"Efficient Water Management - Guidelines for Business",
CBI, London, UK

CBI (1993)
"Energy Management - Good for Business and Good for the Environment",
CBI, London, UK

CBI (1993)
"Reducing the Burden of Waste - Guidelines for Business",
CBI, London, UK

CBI (1994)
"Environmental Education and Training - Guidelines for Business",
CBI, London, UK

Chemical Industries Association (1993)
"Chemicals in a Sustainable World: Responsible Care",
Chemical Industries Association, London, UK

Deloitte Touche Tohmatsu International, International Institute for Sustainable Development, and SustainAbility (1993)
"Coming Clean: Corporate Environmental Reporting: Opening up for Sustainable Development",
Touche Ross Management Consultants, London, UK

Department of the Environment (1990)
"Clean Technology",
DOE, London, UK

Department of the Environment (1991)
"Guide to the Environmental Protection Act",
DOE, London, UK

Department of the Environment (1991)
"Integrated Pollution Control - A Practical Guide",
DOE, London, UK

Department of the Environment (1991)
"Waste Management - The Duty of Care: A Code of Practice",
DOE, London, UK

Department of Trade and Industry (1990)
"Cutting Your Losses - A DTI Business Guide to Waste Minimisation",
DTI, London, UK

Department of Trade and Industry (1992)
"Cutting Your Losses 2: A Further Guide to Waste Minimisation for Business",
DTI, London, UK

Department of Trade and Industry (1992)
"Manufacturing and the Environment:An Executive Guide",
DTI, London, UK

Department of Trade and Industry (1992)
"UK Environmental Exporters: One Hundred Success Stories",
DTI, London, UK

Department of Trade and Industry (1994)
"An Introduction to UK Environmental Technologies",
DTI, London, UK

Department of Trade and Industry (1994)
"Environmental contacts: A Guide for Business - Who does what in Government Departments",
DTI, London, UK

Department of Trade and Industry (1994)
"UK Environmental Business Club Directory",
DTI, London, UK

Elkington J, with Burke T (1987)
"The Green Capitalists: Industry's Search for Environmental Excellence",
Victor Gollancz, London, UK

Elkington J, Knight P with Hailes J (1991)
"The Green Business Guide",
Victor Gollancz, London, UK

Elkington J, et al (1988)
"Green Pages: The Business of Saving the World",
Routledge, London, UK

Elkington J, SustainAbility & the World Wide Fund for Nature (1990)
"The Environmental Audit: A Green Filter for Company Policies, Plants, Processes and Products",
SustainAbility, The People's Hall, 91-97 Freston Road, London W11 4BD, UK

The Environment Council (1989)
"Who's Who in the Environment: Scotland",
The Environment Council, London, UK

The Environment Council (1991)
"Who's Who in the Environment: Wales",
The Environment Council, London, UK

The Environment Council (1992)
"Who's Who in the Environment: England",
The Environment Council, London, UK

Global Environmental Management Initiative (1992)
"Environmental Self-Assessment Program based on the ICC's Business Charter for Sustainable Development",
GEMI, Washington DC

Grayson L (1992)
"BS 7750: What the New Environmental Standard Means for Your Business",
Technical Communications (Publishing), Letchworth, in association with the British Library, UK

Hemming C (1993)
"Business Success from Seizing the Environmental Initiative",
Business and the Environment Practitioner Series, Technical Communications (Publishing) Ltd, UK

Hill J (1992)
"Towards Good Environmental Practice - a Book of Case Studies",
The Institute of Business Ethics, London, UK

International Chamber of Commerce (1991)
"ICC Guide to Effective Environmental Auditing",
ICC, Paris, France

International Chamber of Commerce (1991)
"ICC Business Charter for Sustainable Development - Principles of Environmental Management",
ICC, Paris, France

International Chamber of Commerce (1994)
"UK Seminar Report: Examples from Companies of how they are Implementing the Charter [ICC Business Charter for Sustainable Development]",
ICC UNITED KINGDOM, London, UK

Schmidheiny S & The Business Council for Sustainable Development (1992)
"Changing Course: A Business Perspective on Development and the Environment",
Massachusetts Institute of Technology, USA

Smith C, MP & Cook R, MP (1994)
"Key Environmental Opportunities for Industry",
a Labour Party Paper, Labour Party, London, UK

UK Government (1994)
"Sustainable Development -The UK Strategy",
HMSO, London, UK

United Nations Environment Programme (1993)
"Cleaner Production Worldwide",
UNEP Industry and Environment Programme Activity Centre, Paris, France.

Willums J-O & Goluke U (1992)
"From Ideas to Action - Business and Sustainable Development; The Greening of Enterprise 92",
ICC Publishing, Paris, France

World Industry Council for the Environment (1994)
"Environmental Reporting: A Manager's Guide",
WICE, Paris, France

JOURNALS:

CBI Environment Newsletter (quarterly),
Environment Group, CBI, London UK

The ENDS Report (monthly),
Environmental Data Services Ltd, London, UK

Energy Management (bi-monthly),
Energy Efficiency Office, London, UK

EnviroEconomy (monthly),
IFS International Ltd, Bedford, UK

Environment Today (quarterly),
Brodie Publishing Ltd, Liverpool, UK

Greenpeace Business (bi-monthly),
Greenpeace Ltd, London, UK

APPENDIX 4

Glossary

★ Denotes words that appear elsewhere in the glossary

Biological Oxygen Demand (BOD)
The amount of oxygen used by micro-organisms per unit volume of water at a given temperature, for a given time. It is used as a measure of water pollution caused by organic materials.

Biodegradable
Capable of being decomposed by bacteria or other biological means.

BREEAM
Building Research Establishment Environmental Assessment Method.
This is a method of assessing the environmental quality of buildings, covering issues such as global atmospheric pollution, depletion of material resources, local environment, safety and security.

BS 5750 Quality Systems
The British Standard Institution's award for the management of quality.

BS 7750
The new British Standard for Environmental Management Systems. The Standard is to encourage organisations to establish an effective management system, as a foundation for sound environmental performance and participation in environmental auditing schemes.

Carbon dioxide (CO_2)
Gas present in the atmosphere and formed during respiration, the decomposition and combustion of organic compounds (e.g. fossil fuels, wood). A greenhouse gas★ - therefore it may contribute to global warming★.

Carbon monoxide (CO)
A toxic colourless gas produced by the incomplete combustion of carbon, mainly from combustion of petrol.

Chlorofluorocarbons (CFCs)
Compounds of carbon, chlorine and fluorine. Until the late 1980s, widely used in aerosols, solvents, refrigerants and in foam making. They destroy the ozone layer and their production and use is to be phased out by the end of 1994 under the Montreal Protocol. They are also greenhouse gases★.

CHP
Combined Heat and Power, meaning power stations and generating plants that provide both heat and electricity. The heat - hot water and/or steam - must be used locally.

Cradle to grave
Refers to the responsibility of manufacturers to be concerned with every aspect of product design and use - from the environmental impact of the raw materials to their disposal, re-use or recycling.

Dioxins
Produced when chlorinated materials, such as PVC, are burned at low temperature. Highly toxic to animals, they may cause cancer in humans.

Duty of care
Requires that a company demonstrates it has taken all reasonable precautions to ensure that all waste is disposed of in a responsible fashion by a registered waste carrier in licensed disposal sites.

Eco-labelling
A European Union initiative for consumer products showing which products meet high environmental criteria.

Eco-Management and Audit
A voluntary European Union scheme to encourage environmental management in industry.

Environmental Impact Assessment
A formal assessment of the total environmental effect of a project, process, product or development.

Giga joules
One thousand million or 10^9 joules. A joule is a unit of work or energy.

Global warming
The increase in the average temperature of the earth, thought to be caused by the build up of greenhouse gases★, in particular carbon dioxide★ from fossil fuel burning and methane★.
The gases behave, in effect, like glass in a greenhouse; glass allows solar radiation in, which heats the interior, but reduces the outward emission of heat radiation.

Greenhouse effect
See Global warming★

Greenhouse gases	Naturally occurring gases, such as carbon dioxide*, nitrous oxide, methane* and ozone, and man-made gases like CFCs*, which absorb some of the sun's radiation and convert it into heat.
Hydrochlorofluorocarbons (HCFCs)	Used as replacements to CFCs* in refrigeration, foam blowing and aerosols. HCFCs are slower to deplete the ozone layer* than CFCs*. They also contribute to the build-up of greenhouse gases*.
Hydrofluorocarbons (HFCs)	Halogenated carbons, similar to HCFCs*. They do not contain chlorine and are not, therefore, ozone depleting, but contribute to the build-up of greenhouse gases*.
Her Majesty's Inspectorate of Pollution (HMIP)	Responsible for regulating the most serious polluting industrial processes under the Environment Protection Act 1990. (See Appendix Two - Further Information).
Integrated Pollution Control (IPC)	Created by the 1990 Environmental Protection Act and regulated by HMIP*. IPC is an approach to pollution control in the UK, which looks at the environment as a whole so that solutions to particular pollution problems take account of potential effects upon water, land and air.
ISO 9000	International Standards Organisation quality systems standard.
Leaching	Loss of soluble substances from a solid mass, e.g. soil, by the action of percolating liquid.
Life Cycle Analysis	A technique to examine the entire life of a product, from the extraction of raw materials to manufacture to disposal.
Methane (CH_4)	The simplest member of the hydrocarbon family. Methane is a potent greenhouse gas*.
Nitrogen oxides (NO_x)	A range of compounds formed by the oxidation of atmospheric nitrogen. Some of these oxides contribute to acid rain and smog, and can affect the stratospheric ozone layer*.
Non-Fossil Fuel Obligation (NFFO)	Listed under the Electricity Act 1989, the Obligation in the form of Orders is the Government's main instrument for pursuing a figure of 1,500 MW of new renewable electricity generating capacity in the UK by the year 2000.
Organochlorines	Any organic compound containing chlorine, e.g. PCBs* and pesticides such as DDT and lindane.
Oxidation	Usually a chemical reaction with oxygen, producing oxides.
Ozone Layer	A layer of ozone in the upper atmosphere (the stratosphere) that protects the earth from harmful ultra-violet radiation.
Polychlorinated biphenyls (PCBs)	A group of widely used compounds containing chlorine. PCBs can accumulate in food chains and at high concentrations are thought likely to produce harmful side effects, particularly during the reproductive cycle of some marine animals.
Site of Special Scientific Interest (SSSI)	Notified under the Wildlife and Countryside Act 1981, the site is recognised for its special biological and/or geological interest.
Special waste	Controlled waste which consists of, or contains, substances which are "dangerous to life" as defined in UK regulations.
Sulphur dioxide (SO_2)	A compound of sulphur and oxygen which is emitted into the atmosphere by the combustion of fuels containing sulphur, such as coal, diesel oil and fuel oil. It is toxic at high concentrations and contributes to acidity in rain.
Sulphur Oxides (SO_x)	A range of compounds formed by the oxidation* of sulphur, includes sulphur dioxide*.
Sustainable Development	A widely quoted definition from the 1987 report of the World Commission on Environment and Development: development that meets the needs of the present without compromising the ability of future generations to meet their own needs.
Sustainability	See Sustainable Development.
Volatile Organic Compounds (VOCs)	Result from the use of petrol solvents, paints and degreasing agents in industry. They evaporate readily and contribute to air pollution mainly through the production of secondary pollutants such as ozone.

APPENDIX 5

Other Publications of
the Institute of Business Ethics

WHAT'S ALL THIS ABOUT BUSINESS ETHICS?

An Occasional Paper by Neville Cooper, Chairman of the Institute of Business
Ethics. He starts by quoting the cynics who wonder if there is such a thing and goes
on to argue that business is a fundamentally ethical activity, but clearly subject to
abuse, arising from fraud, misuse of power, exploitation and so on. The paper
examines briefly some of the main ethical issues and explains why the IBE was
founded.

ISBN 0 9513671 1 0   Price £2.95

BUSINESS AND SOCIETY - THE APPROACH OF THE FAITHS

An Occasional Paper based on a conference involving speakers from the three
religions which support the aims of the IBE - Christian, Muslim and Jewish. It
shows how much common ground there is and how the different religions should
learn from each other on such key questions as investments, debt, profits and
wealth creation.

ISBN 0 9513671 2 9   Price £3.50

COMPANY PHILOSOPHIES AND CODES OF BUSINESS ETHICS

This Guide by Simon Webley is based on a conference on the subject run by the
IBE, following replies from 100 companies to a survey on existing practice.
It makes the case for such standards, discusses key subjects such as bribery, use of
privileged information and conflicts of interest. It includes a model statement of
business principles and an outline code as well as examples of existing codes.

ISBN 0 9513671 0 2   Price £7.50

BUSINESS ETHICS AND COMPANY CODES

A Report by Simon Webley which updates the previous publication "Company
Philosophies and Codes of Business Ethics". It sets out the principal ways in which
companies translate their ethical values into practice through the promulgation of
codes throughout their work force. It draws on existing practice by leading
companies and includes a short form code which can be used as the basis for
companies wishing to develop codes of their own.

ISBN 0 9513671 7 X   Price £15.00

PERSONAL DEBT - IS IT TOO MUCH ENCOURAGED?

A Report on a Conference on a very difficult and highly relevant topic, affecting as it does the relationship between corporate lenders and private borrowers. Speakers represented all sides of the argument.

ISBN 0 9513671 3 7   Price £7.50

MANAGEMENT AND THE HEALTH OF EMPLOYEES

A Report on a Conference addressed by speakers from two industries very different in size, one from BUPA and a Jesuit priest. They went beyond health, safety and environmental management issues, being concerned with giving individuals a sense of their own value, encouraging their development and avoiding stress: some useful insights into the basic principles of how to manage people.

ISBN 0 9513671 6 1   Price £9.00

TAKEOVERS - WHAT ETHICAL CONSIDERATIONS SHOULD APPLY?

A Report on a Conference on this difficult and topical subject, which was addressed by the chairman of the Takeover Panel, a former company chairman, a management consultant and a merchant banker.

ISBN 0 9513671 4 5   Price £7.50

ETHICS, ENVIRONMENT AND THE COMPANY

This Guide for Effective Action was written by Tom Burke and Julie Hill of the Green Alliance. It covers one of the most important challenges to management of the 1990s, which companies will ignore at their peril. It gives the results of replies from 82 companies to a survey of their existing practices in this field and makes practical recommendations for environmental management for adoption by businesses of every size and type.

ISBN 0 9513671 5 3   Price £10.00

TOWARDS GOOD ENVIRONMENTAL PRACTICE

This is an in-depth, practical follow-up to the earlier publications "Ethics, Environment and the Company". Julie Hill of the Green Alliance has compiled case studies from nine UK companies of widely different sizes and types of business. These illustrate very different approaches and degrees of success in developing policies and practices aimed at achieving environmental improvement. Invaluable to practitioners, teachers and students.

ISBN 0 9513671 8 8   Price £20.00

CODES OF BUSINESS ETHICS

This check-list and illustrative code by Simon Webley gives a list of 62 subjects involving business ethics, a code which can form the basis for any company to use and a list of larger companies in the UK, known to the Institute to have codes of business ethics.

ISBN 0 9513671 9 6   Price £10.00

Sponsored by the Department of the Environment

Designed & produced by Designline, Havant

Price £24.00

Paper supplied by: **Paper Back**
Printed on: Sylvancoat - *45% woodfree unprinted waste, 45% woodfree printed waste &10% virgin fibre.*